COUNTRY WEEKEND
PATCHWORK QUILTS

26 Quilts To Make
with Time-Saving Shortcuts
and Techniques

By Leslie Linsley

Photographs by Jon Aron

Sedgewood® Press
New York, N.Y.

DEDICATION

To all the women in my life who mean the most to me: my daughters Lisa McCandless, Amy Shaffer, and Robby Smith; my mother Ruth Linsley; my grandmother Anna Zuckerman; my mother-in-law Sade Aron; and the many aunts who make up my extended family.

ACKNOWLEDGEMENT

I'm especially grateful for the wonderful Nantucket homes and gardens made available to us by our neighbors for photographing the quilts in this book. Special thanks to Mr. and Mrs. Scott Stearns and to Lee Gaw for allowing us access to the beautiful rooms in her country inn, Fair Gardens.

I'd also like to thank Avis Skinner of Nantucket, Massachusetts, for sharing some of the nicest quilts from her collection at Vis-à-Vis, and Janet Russo, also of Nantucket, for the quilts from her collection. Also thanks, to Lynn Knight for sharing her quilts.

And finally, I appreciate having had the good fortune to work with a caring and very professional editor, Constance Schrader.

CREDITS

Illustrations
Robby Smith
Peter Peluso, Jr.
Photographs of the Wool Coverlet on page 39 and the Homespun Table Cover on page 140 courtesy *Family Circle* magazine.

FOR SEDGEWOOD PRESS

Director: Elizabeth P. Rice
Project Editor: Viviene Fauerbach
Assistant: Ruth Weadock
Production Manager: Bill Rose
Design: Remo Cosentino/Bookgraphics

Distributed by Meredith Corporation, Des Moines, Iowa.
ISBN: 0-696-02334-2
Library of Congress Catalog Card 89-061410

Printed in the United States of America

10 9 8 7 6 5 4 3 2 1

CONTENTS

INTRODUCTION   5

GETTING STARTED IN QUILTING

Quilting Terms   9
Materials for Quilting   10
Quilting Techniques   12
Quick-and-Easy Methods   16
Sewing Tips   18

WEEKEND QUILTS

Card Trick   20
Fair and Square   26
Blue and White Missouri Star   32
Wool Coverlet   38
Roman Stripes   42
Maze of Grays   48
Baby Stripes   54
Harlequin Squares   58
LeMoyne Star   63
Baby Blocks   70
Log Cabin Wall Hanging   76
Pinwheel Star   82
Jacob's Ladder   89
Amish 9 Patch   95
Barn Raising   100
Wedding Wreath   107
White on White   113
Bear Claw   118
Summer Coverlet   124
Kaleidoscope   129
Tic Tac Toe   134
Homespun Table Cover   139
Roses and Bows   143
Irish Chain   148
Stripes and Solids   154
Handy Andy   159

INDEX   167

Dear Quilter:

So many of us are busy, and the busier we get, the more we want quick and easy projects. Leslie Linsley's COUNTRY WEEKEND PATCHWORK QUILTS is the result of years of effort to capture the beauty of traditional quilt designs while using quick-and-easy shortcut techniques.

Leslie has adapted standard methods of cutting and piecing, and added some of her own ideas. For example, *Jacob's Ladder*, a charming combination of blue and white in a French provincial print, shown on the cover and on page 90, uses both the quick-and-easy triangle method and the strip-piecing technique. These devices eliminate hours of work, allowing you to create this intricate-looking quilt, with its companion pillows, in a few short days.

Since 1982, Sedgewood® Press has been dedicated to bringing you quality craft books with both traditional and unusual designs, clear directions, and color photographs of all projects. Proud as we may be of our books, our success depends on your success in making the project of your choice. We hope you will enjoy COUNTRY WEEKEND PATCHWORK QUILTS, and will use it happily to create your own quilts. We look forward to bringing you other craft and needlework books, and we hope you look forward to new Sedgewood books.

Sincerely yours,

Connie Schrader

Connie Schrader
Editorial Project Manager

INTRODUCTION

Nothing suggests country decorating as well as the addition of a patchwork quilt to a room. Whether it's a quilt on the bed, over a sofa, or hanging on a wall, quilts make a room homey and cozy. However, while we'd all like to fill our homes with wonderful handmade quilts, few of us have the time to devote to such a long-term project. In fact, the busier we get, the more we want quick-and-easy projects. That's why the idea for piecing a quilt in a weekend is so appealing.

For the past few years my husband and partner Jon Aron, who is a graphic designer, my daughter Robby, who is also a designer, and I have been creating designs as well as looking for beautiful old quilts with patterns that can be reproduced with a minimum of preparation and piecing time. *Country Weekend Patchwork Quilts* is the result. I think you'll find that each of the quilts presented here can be made with the quick-and-easy shortcut techniques that we've adapted from traditional methods of quilting and with new ideas that we've created to make piecing a cinch.

For example, there is a nice variety of basic patchwork quilt designs to choose from. Beginning with a simple one-patch pattern, you can learn how to combine different fabric squares for a pieced quilt top that is both interesting and easy to do.

Sewing strips is the basic technique for making quilt blocks out of rectangles and squares, and you'll find several quilts using this method. Complex patterns can be developed from simple arrangements of strips that are cut into squares and then pieced.

You'll be introduced to the quick-and-easy right triangle method and learn how to combine squares and triangles in order to easily expand design possibilities. You'll also learn how to make new and interesting versions of familiar and much-loved early American country quilts. These are patterns that quilt lovers want to preserve as part of our heritage. In keeping with the quick-and-easy theme, each of these patterns is doable in a weekend. I think you'll find that the fresh choice of fabric colors and their placement give each design a new look.

I've introduced the use of large fabric prints. We've developed and used this technique recently to create very elegant, but supersimple, quilts. The use of a large print is the key element. By using the full print as the quilt block and combining it with solid squares, the piecing becomes very quick-and-easy. Further, setting each block on the diagonal creates a dramatic effect. Time not spent on the piecing of small patches can be applied to the quilting. A contrasting border often adds to the design. Our Roses and Bows quilt on page 143 has the added interest of a tied effect from the fabric bows applied to the center of each solid square. This project was inspired by the earliest English quilts. Yet, because of the fabric, it should appeal to modern-day quilters.

If you can sew a straight seam on a sewing machine, you'll be able to stitch any of these quilts in a weekend. Robby has worked out the step-by-step diagrams to go with the directions so that you have, not only complete written instructions, but a good visual sequence to refer to as you work. In this way, if you have a basic understanding of the quilting process, for some of the steps you can easily refer to the diagrams alone, thus making the piecing that much easier.

The reference material provides you with the basics of the quilting process and furnishes information about the materials. It's here that you'll also find quick-and-easy shortcuts and suggestions. Because these suggestions are not always repeated with each project, it's a good idea to read this introductory section before you start working.

I've written several quilt books, and I try to add something new to the reference material of each new book. The longer I do this, the more I learn, and this makes me anxious to write the next book so I can pass along the newfound information. I especially enjoy sharing tips that have been sent to me by readers or that I've discovered from my own reading. So, at the end of the reference section, you'll find my latest offering of time-saving, practical tips that are fun to read and incorporate wherever applicable.

And now a word about decorating with quilts. I don't have to tell you that home decorating has become a popular pastime. More than ever before, we seem to care about how our homes reflect our lifestyles. Country decorating is here to stay. And no wonder! It's a style that we're all comfortable with, having evolved from our very own heritage. I've been especially interested in incorporating quilts into all styles of decorating. Quilts make wonderful accessories that are attractive and practical and they work well in a traditional as well as in a contemporary home. Best of all, anyone can make a quilt.

Throughout the book, you'll find quilts shown in various settings. It is my purpose to show you how attractive a quilt can be when used as a wall hanging, on a table, or as a bed cover. Many smaller quilts, which I call throws or coverlets, are perfect for folding over the back of a sofa. This adds to our country decorating and is practical for chilly evenings as well.

A quilt is also right at home in the nursery, and since quilts always get better with repeated washings and wear, this is a most practical project for the new baby. Best of all, you can make a small-size quilt before mother and newborn even come home from the hospital. A quilt is the perfect baby shower gift. It's so personal and always appreciated. This is also a good project for two people to make as a joint gift. One person does the machine piecing and the other does the hand quilting.

In our family, Robby likes to do the piecing and I prefer the handwork. The Irish Chain on page 148, which Robby designed, is just such a project. There's only one problem: Each of us claims the quilt as our own and we constantly argue over who should own it. I guess we'll have to give it to one of Robby's sisters and hope it will become a family heirloom. And that's another aspect of quiltmaking: The process is enjoyable. Quilts look sensational wherever you use them. They're appreciated as a very special gift. They get better with age. They even increase in value, although they are basically inexpensive to make. And they become family heirlooms. I really can't think of another craft that has such appeal. Happy quilting!

L.L.

GETTING STARTED IN QUILTING

Whether you're a beginner or have been making quilts for a long time, I always recommend reading over the quilting terms and basic directions for using the materials. In this way, before starting one of the projects, you'll have an idea of what's involved and can evaluate the project in terms of skill and materials needed.

Even if you're an old hand at quilting, skim through the following material. It will be a helpful refresher course. I always reread my previous books to see how I can improve on what I've already learned. I've added this information here to make quiltmaking more pleasurable for you.

QUILTING TERMS

Before starting a project, I always recommend learning the basic terms and crafting skills so that you'll be able to understand the different processes and become familiar with the different kinds of quilts. When you look at a patchwork quilt, you'll know how it was made. Knowing what's involved will help you decide which project you'd like to make first. Also, the directions will be clearer. They are basic and logical and, if you are new to the craft, they will enable you to make a quilt.

Backing: The piece of fabric used on the underside of the pieced or appliquéd top. Usually of the same weight fabric, this piece can be made from solid or printed fabric to match the design on the top of the quilt. Sometimes the backing is made from the same fabric as that which is used to create the borders on the quilt top. I especially like to use an old sheet for the backing. The size is large enough without adding seams for piecing, and an old sheet is nice and soft.

Basting: Long, loose stitches used to hold the top, batting, and backing together before quilting. These stitches are removed after each section is quilted.

Batting: The soft lining that makes the quilt puffy and gives it warmth. Batting comes in various thicknesses, each appropriate for different kinds of projects. Most quilts are made with a thin layer of Traditional Poly-Fil. Batting also comes in small, fluffy pieces that are used for stuffing projects, such as sachets, pin cushions, pillows, and so on.

Binding: The way the raw edges of fabric are finished. Many quiltmakers cut the backing slightly larger than the top piece so they can bring the extra fabric forward to finish the edges. Contrasting fabric or bias binding is also used.

Block: Geometric or symmetrical pieces of fabric sewn together to create a design. The finished blocks are sewn together to create the finished quilt top. Individual blocks are often large enough to be used for a matching pillow.

Borders: Fabric strips that frame the pieced design. A border can be narrow or wide, and sometimes there is more than one border around a quilt. Borders often frame quilt blocks and are sometimes made from one of the fabrics or from a contrasting fabric. Borders are often used to enlarge a quilt top so that it extends over the sides of the mattress.

Traditionally, for the sake of interest, quilting patterns are stitched in the borders. However, many quilters leave this area free of stitches in order to complete the project in a shorter period of time.

Patchwork: Fabric pieces sewn together to create an entire design. Sometimes the shapes form a geometric block. The blocks are then sewn together to make up the completed quilt.

Piecing: Joining patchwork pieces together to form a design on the block.

Quilting: Stitching together two layers of fabric with a layer of batting between them.

Quilting patterns: The lines or markings on the fabric that make up the design. Small hand or machine stitches quilt along these lines, which might be straight, curved, or made up of elaborate curlicued patterns. Small quilting stitches can also follow the seam lines where pieces of fabric are joined. Or, a quilting pattern can be created by stitching a grid or diamonds over the entire fabric.

Sash or strips: The narrow pieces of fabric used to frame the individual blocks and join them together. They are often used in a contrasting color.

Setting: Joining the quilt blocks to form the finished top of the quilt.

Top: The top of a quilting project is the front layer of fabric with the right side showing. Patchwork or appliquéd pieces create the top fabric.

MATERIALS FOR QUILTING

Fabric: You can never have too many different fabric patterns when designing a quilting project. I always seem to need ten times more variety to choose from than I think. Fabric is the main concern: what kind, how much to buy, and what colors or prints will work together.

Almost every type of fabric has been used for making quilts and quilting projects. However, most quilters prefer cotton and, if necessary, will settle for a cotton/polyester blend in order to find the right color or pattern for the project. All fabric, but especially pure cotton, should be washed before it is used. This removes any sizing in the fabric and allows for shrinkage before making the project. Sometimes cotton fabric fades slightly. This produces a worn, old look which is desirable in the world of quiltmaking.

When collecting a variety of fabric prints for your quilting projects, it's a good idea to have a selection of lights and darks. The colors and patterns of the fabric will greatly affect the design. Calico has always been used for quilting projects. The small, overall prints can be used effectively together, and there is a wide variety of colors to choose from.

Needles: All of the projects in this book are pieced on a sewing machine. The quilting can be done by hand or on the machine, but hand quilting looks best. If the batting is Extra-Loft, it will not go through the machine and the quilting must be done by hand. To do this, buy #7 and #8 sharps which are the most common size needles used for hand quilting. They are often called "betweens."

Thread: Match the thread to the color of the fabric. Cotton-blend thread is best for all quilting and piecing.

Scissors: Good-quality scissors are a must. They are essential for accurately cutting your fabric. *Do not use your fabric scissors for cutting paper.* This will ruin your scissors.

Thimble: I used to be averse to using a thimble. Every time I started out with one I would eventually abandon it. This year I've been doing a lot more hand quilting than usual, however, and my fingers are a mess from needle pricks. I have therefore reformed, and now recommend a thimble for all hand quilting. Be sure to get the right size. It makes all the difference in the world.

If you are making a project with hand-sewn stitches, you will be taking three to six stitches at a time through three layers of fabric. A thimble can make this task painless and more fun.

Template: A rigid, full-size pattern that is used to trace design elements. It can be cut from cardboard, manila oaktag used for filing folders, plastic, or acetate. Acetate, which is transparent and produces clean, crisp edges, should be used for pattern pieces when a repeat design is required. Sandpaper is also a good material for templates because it doesn't slip when placed facedown on fabric. If you are cutting one design, you can simply use the paper pattern pinned to the fabric as a cutting guide.

When the pattern piece for any project in this book calls for a template, the directions will note whether a seam allowance is included. If not, add ¼ inch for seam allowance when cutting fabric with a template.

Markers: Sometimes a pattern or design has to be traced from the book and transferred to the fabric. When you want an overall quilting design, you'll need lines to follow. Water-soluble marking pens are sold in fabric shops. These pens are used to mark quilting lines on the fabric. After all stitching is complete, the pen marks can be removed with a plant mister or damp sponge. Simply pat over the lines and they disappear.

Iron: It's impossible to work on any project without having an iron right next to the sewing machine. After each stitching direction, you will be instructed to press the fabric. If you are doing patchwork, it's handy to pad a stool or chair with a piece of batting and place it next to you by the sewing machine. As you piece the fabric, you can iron the seams without getting up. Use a steam setting.

Cutting board: This is a handy item for quick measuring and cutting methods you'll use for making quilts. It is available in fabric stores or from mail-order sources.

Ruler and yardstick: You can't work without them. A metal ruler can be used as a straight edge for the most accurate cutting. Use the yardstick for cutting lengths of fabric where you must mark and cut at least 36 inches at one time.

The width of the yardstick is perfect for marking a grid pattern for quilting. You simply draw the first line, then flip the yardstick over and continue to mark lines without ever removing the yardstick from the fabric. You will have a perfect 1-inch grid.

QUILTING TECHNIQUES

Estimating fabric yardage

The fabric used for all of these projects is 45 inches wide. All measurements are figured with a ¼-inch seam allowance unless otherwise specified.

Every project lists the exact amount of material needed for each color, and all the quilt projects are made to fit standard bed sizes, which are given with each project. However, you may want to be sure that a specific quilt will fit your special needs, or you might want to change the size specified to something larger or smaller. It's easy to figure what size will best fit your bed.

When estimating yardage for a bed quilt, measure your bed fully made. This means with bed pad, sheets, and blankets over the mattress.

Measure the length, width, and depth, including the box spring. Decide if you want a slight overhang, an overhang to the top of a dust ruffle, or a drop to the floor, and whether or not the quilt will extend up and over the pillows. If a quilt size for any project isn't the right size for your bed, it can be changed by adding to, or subtracting from, the border measurements. This shouldn't change the basic design.

Piecing the backing

You may have to piece panels together for the back of a quilt, tablecloth, or wall hanging in order to get the correct size. Use the full width of fabric, (usually 45 inches) cut to the appropriate length. Cut another piece the same size. Then cut the second strip of fabric in half lengthwise so that you have two narrow strips of the same size. Join these two matching panels to each long-sided edge of the large center panel to avoid a seam down the middle of the quilt backing. Press seams open.

Enlarging designs

Most patterns and designs are shown full size, but sometimes they are too large to fit on a page. In this case, the designs are shown on a grid for easy enlargement. Each square on the grid equals 1 inch. This means that you will transfer or copy the design onto graph paper marked with 1-inch squares. Begin by counting the number of squares on the pattern in the book. Number them horizontally and again vertically. Count the number of squares on your larger graph and number them in the same way. Copy the design onto your grid one square at a time.

Transferring a large design

Trace the pattern pieces or quilting design from the book. Place a piece of dressmaker's tracing (carbon) paper on the right side of the fabric with the carbon side down and tracing paper on top. Go over all pattern lines with a tracing wheel or ballpoint pen to transfer the design. Remove the carbon and tracing.

Making a template

Transfer the pattern to the template material by first tracing the design. Place the tracing facedown on the cardboard and using a pen or pencil, rub over each traced line. The outline will be transferred to the cardboard. Remove the tracing and go over the lines with a ballpoint pen to make them legible. Cut out the design outline from the card-board. If using acetate, simply place it over the tracing and cut out the exact shape.

Determine which fabric will be used for each template. Place the templates at least ½ inch apart to allow for the ¼-inch seam allowance when cutting out each piece. You may even want to allow for ⅜-inch seams for each turning of the edges. This will be determined by the thickness of the fabric, whether or not the design has points, curves, and so on. Try both space allowances to see which works for you.

Consider the grain of the fabric and the direction of the print when placing your templates.

Sewing points

Many traditional quilt patterns are created from triangles, diamonds, and similar shapes. The points present a challenge and require special care.

When stitching 2 such pieces together, sew along the stitch line, but do not sew into the seam allowance at each point. It helps to mark the finished points with a pin so that you can begin and end your seams at these marks.

Sewing curves

Before turning a curved appliqué piece, stay-stitch along the seam line, then clip or notch evenly spaced cuts along the edge in the seam allowance. Clip all inward curves and notch all outward curves. When the fabric is turned under, it will lie flat.

Sewing inside corner edge

Place a pin across the point of the stitches and clip up to the stitches in the seam allowance in order to turn the fabric under.

Outside corner edge

Once you've stitched around a corner, clip off half the seam allowance across the point. Turn fabric back, press seams open, and trim excess fabric away.

Turning corners

It's often a bit difficult to turn corners and continue a seam line. Figure 1 shows the 3 pieces to be joined. With right sides facing, stitch

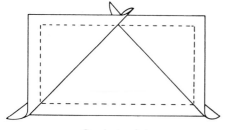

Sewing points

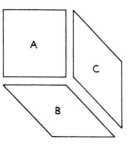

Figure 1

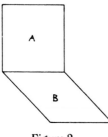

Figure 2

14

piece A to piece B as shown in Figure 2. Next, join C to A, as shown in Figure 3. Leave the needle down in fabric. Lift the presser foot and clip the seam to the needle. Slide B under C and adjust so the edges of B align with C. Lower the presser foot and stitch along the seam line (see Figure 4).

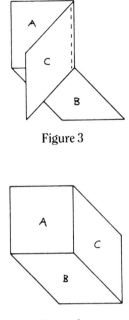

Figure 3

How to quilt

Quilting is sewing layers of fabric and batting together to produce a padded fabric held together by stitching. The quilting process, generally the finishing step in a patchwork project, is what makes the project interesting and gives it a textured look.

Basting

Before quilting, you will have to baste the quilt top, batting, and backing together. To avoid a lump of filler at any point, begin at the center of the top and baste outward with long, loose stitches, to create a sunburst pattern. There should be about 6 inches between the basted lines at the edges of the quilt. Baste from the top only. These stitches will be cut away as you do your quilting.

Figure 4

Hand quilting

Thread your needle and knot one end as you would for regular hand sewing. Bring the needle up through the back to the front and give the knotted end a good tug to pull it through the backing fabric into the batting. Keep your thread fairly short (about 18 inches) and take small running stitches. Follow your premarked quilting pattern or stitch ¼ inch on each side of all seam lines. Do not stitch into the ¼-inch seam allowance around the outside edge of the quilt.

Machine quilting

This quicker way to create a quilted look does not have the same, rich look of authentic, early quilting that hand stitching does. It is best to machine quilt when the batting isn't too thick. Although the piecing of the quilts can be finished in a weekend, I still recommend hand quilting unless it's more important that the project be completed quickly.

When machine quilting, set the thread tension approximately 6 stitches to the inch so that the stitching looks like hand stitching. Taking this precaution will assure that the absence of hand stitching does not detract from the design.

Outlining

This is the method of quilting along the patchwork seams. In this way, each design element is pronounced and the fabric layers are secured.

Overall quilting

When you want to fill large areas of the background with quilting, choose a simple design. The background quilting should not interfere with the patchwork elements.

To ensure accurate spacing, make grid patterns of squares or diamond shapes with a yardstick or masking tape. For a quick-and-easy method, lay a yardstick diagonally across the fabric and mark the material with a light pencil. Without removing the yardstick, turn it over and mark along the edge once again. Continue across the fabric to the opposite edge. You will have perfect 1-inch spaces between each line. Lay the yardstick across the fabric at the corner opposite where you began and repeat the process to create a 1-inch grid across the top of the fabric. Stitch along these lines. The stitching will hide the pencil lines.

QUICK-AND-EASY METHODS

Strip piecing

This is the method by which you sew strips of different fabrics together and cut them into units that are arranged to make up the entire quilt top. Rather than cutting and sewing individual squares together over and over again, two or more strips of fabric are sewn together and then cut into segments that are the exact same dimensions. These units are then arranged and stitched together in different positions to form the quilt pattern.

Right triangles

There is a quick-and-easy way to join light and dark triangles to create squares of any size. Once you've determined the size of your finished unit, add 1 inch to it. For example, if you want to create 2-inch squares, mark off 3-inch squares on the wrong side of the light fabric. Next, draw diagonal lines through each square as shown in Figure 1. With right sides facing and raw edges aligned, pin the marked light fabric to the same size dark fabric. Stitch a ¼-inch seam on each side of the drawn diagonal lines as shown.

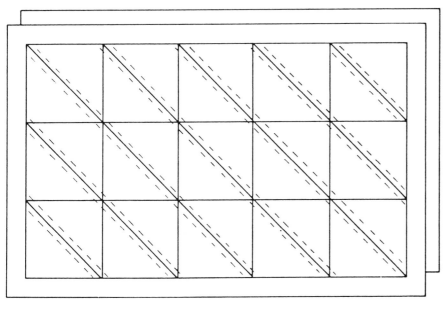

Figure 1

Cut on all solid lines to get the individual squares of light and dark, or contrasting fabric triangles. Open seams and press.

Hanging a quilt

Only quilts that are in good condition and not too heavy should be hung. There are two reliable methods for hanging a quilt or wall hanging. I prefer using a Velcro™ strip, which is effective if the quilt or wall hanging is lightweight and not too large. For this method, machine stitch one side of the Velcro to a strip of cotton tape which is then sewn to the back, top edge of the quilt. Stitch the tape to the backing fabric and batting only, not through to the quilt top, and stop short of each end. The matching side of the Velcro is then applied to a length of lath (available in lumber yards) slightly shorter than the width of the quilt. Attach the quilt to the lath and then mount on the wall. You may want to attach the bottom of the quilt in the same way.

Another method is preferable for heavier quilts. Make a fabric sleeve approximately 3½ to 4 inches deep and an inch shorter than the quilt on each end. Sew it to the back of the quilt, again stitching through the backing and batting, but not to the quilted top side. You can then insert a thin piece of wood through the sleeve and attach it at each end to the wall. Or, you can insert a dowel slightly larger than the quilt. Attach an eyelet to each end of the dowel for hanging.

SEWING TIPS

I've been collecting sewing tips that I'd like to pass along to you. If you have some ideas or shortcuts that you'd like to share, I'd really like to hear from you. Just send them to me at my studio: Nantucket, Massachusetts 02554.

1. To continue hand quilting without interruption, thread several needles at a time and weave them through a woven place mat. As you run out of thread from one needle, switch to the next. When not in use, the place mat can be rolled up easily for storage in a drawer with other supplies.

2. To stitch a perfectly straight line, place a piece of masking tape on the fabric and stitch alongside the edge.

3. To keep sewing fabric clean and visible, store it in clear plastic sweater boxes.

4. To pick up spilled pins quickly, place a nylon stocking over the vacuum suction nozzle and go over the floor. Hold the nozzle over the pin box, turn off the vacuum, and the pins will fall into the box.

5. To thread a needle with ease, stiffen the end of the thread with clear nail polish.

6. The acetate lids of stationery boxes are excellent for making patchwork and appliqué templates.

7. Shavings from a pencil sharpener are terrific for filling a pin cushion and will keep the pins sharpened.

8. Cut pattern pieces out of wax-coated freezer paper and place them facedown on the back of your fabric. Pressing lightly with a warm iron will make the paper adhere so that you can cut the pieces without using pins or basting.

9. To remove pencil marks from quilts, use an art-gum eraser.

10. All cutting directions for the quilts in this book list the pieces in the order in which they should be cut, but here is a reminder: To cut the pattern pieces from the fabric in the most efficient way, cut the border strips first, then fit the other pieces on the remaining fabric. In this way the borders will be cut as one continuous strip and you won't have to piece them.

COUNTRY
WEEKEND
PATCHWORK
QUILTS

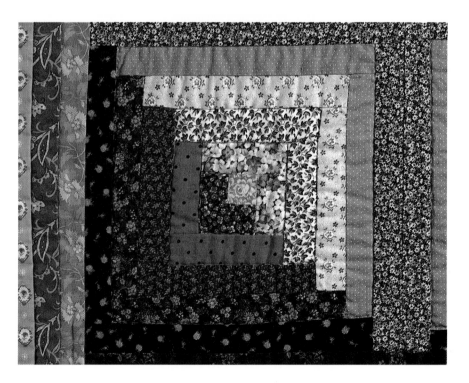

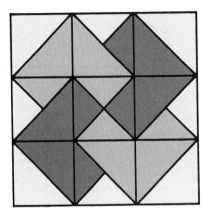

CARD TRICK

A bit unusual, this quilt pattern looks more complicated than it is. I have used this design to make a wall hanging, a table runner, a holiday tablecloth, and a quilt. It's a versatile pattern that can be adapted to many sizes. Here it's shown as a wall hanging measuring 56 × 56 inches. The fabric is from the Provence line of Waverly Fabrics, a division of F. Schumacher and Company, and is available through fabric shops. However, any attractive dark and light prints can be used with a contrasting solid fabric for the lattice strips.

MATERIALS

Note: Yardages are figured for fabric 45 inches wide.

¾ yard tan fabric (A)
¾ yard light calico (B)
¾ yard green calico (C)
1¾ yards rust-colored fabric
3¼ yards backing fabric
thin quilt batting
Velcro tabs or strips for hanging

DIRECTIONS

Note: All measurements include a ¼-inch seam allowance.

Cut the following

from tan (A):

> 18 squares, each 6 × 6 inches; cut each square into 2
> triangles (36 triangles)
> 18 squares, each 4½ × 4½ inches; cut each square into
> 2 triangles (36 triangles)

from light calico (B):

> 18 squares, each 6 × 6 inches; cut each square into 2
> triangles (36 triangles)
> 18 squares, each 4½ × 4½ inches; cut each square into
> 2 triangles (36 triangles)

from green calico (C):

> 18 squares, each 6 × 6 inches; cut each square into 2
> triangles (36 triangles)
> 18 squares, each 4½ × 4½ inches; cut each square into
> 2 triangles (36 triangles)

from rust color:

> borders—
>
> 2 strips, each 3½ × 56½ inches
> 2 strips, each 3½ × 50½ inches
> 2 lattice strips, each 3 × 50½ inches
> 6 lattice strips, each 3 × 15½ inches

To make block units

Refer to Figure 1 throughout.

Unit 1

With right sides facing and raw edges aligned, stitch a large A triangle to a large B triangle along the diagonal to make a square. Open seams and press. Make 18.

Unit 2

With right sides facing and raw edges aligned, stitch a small A triangle to a small C triangle along one short edge to make a larger triangle.

Next, with right sides facing and raw edges aligned, join the A/C triangle to a large B triangle along the diagonal to make a square. Open seams and press. Make 18.

Unit 3

With right sides facing and raw edges aligned, join a large A triangle to a large C triangle along the diagonal to make a square. Open seams and press. Make 18.

Unit 4

With right sides facing and raw edges aligned, join a small A triangle to a small B triangle to make a large triangle.

Next, with right sides facing and raw edges aligned, stitch the A/B triangle to a large C triangle along the diagonal to make a square. Open seams and press. Make 18.

Unit 5

With right sides facing and raw edges aligned, stitch a small C triangle to a small B triangle along one short edge to make a large triangle.

Next, with right sides facing and raw edges aligned, stitch these two larger triangles together along the diagonal to make a square. Open seams and press. Make 9.

To make a block

Refer to Figure 2 throughout.

Row 1: With right sides facing and raw edges aligned, stitch a Unit 1 to a Unit 2, followed by a Unit 3. Open seams and press.

Row 2: With right sides facing and raw edges aligned, stitch a Unit 4 to a Unit 5, followed by a Unit 4. (Note the change of positioning for the second Unit 4.) Open seams and press.

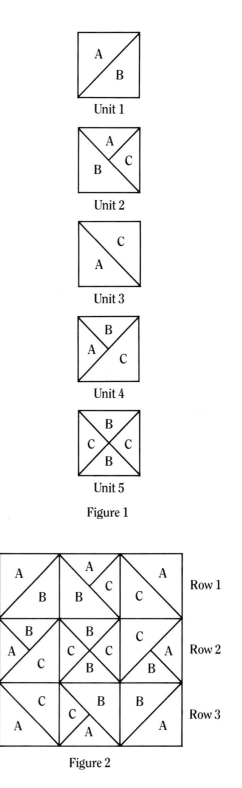

Unit 1

Unit 2

Unit 3

Unit 4

Unit 5

Figure 1

Figure 2

23

Row 3: With right sides facing and raw edges aligned, stitch a Unit 3 to a Unit 2, followed by a Unit 1. (Note the change of positioning for Units 2 and 1.) Open seams and press.

With right sides facing and raw edges aligned, stitch Row 1 of the block to Row 2, followed by Row 3, to complete a block as shown in Figure 2. Open seams and press. Make 9 blocks in this way.

To make a row

1. With right sides facing and raw edges aligned, stitch a block to a $3 \times 15\frac{1}{2}$-inch lattice strip. Open seams and press.

2. Continue to join another block, then a lattice strip, and end the row with another block.

3. Make 3 rows in this way as shown in Figure 3.

Joining rows

Refer to Figure 3.

1. With right sides facing and raw edges aligned, stitch a $3 \times 50\frac{1}{2}$-inch lattice strip to the bottom edge of Row 1. Open seams and press.

2. Continue to join the 3 rows, with a $3 \times 50\frac{1}{2}$-inch lattice strip between each row.

Borders

1. With right sides facing and raw edges aligned, stitch a $3\frac{1}{2} \times 50\frac{1}{2}$-inch border strip to the top edge of the pieced quilt top. Open seams and press. Repeat on the bottom edge.

2. With right sides facing and raw edges aligned, stitch a $3\frac{1}{2} \times 56\frac{1}{2}$-inch strip to one side edge of the quilt top. Open seams and press. Repeat on the opposite side.

To quilt

1. Cut the backing in half and stitch the halves together along the long edge.

2. Pin the top, batting, and backing together. Trim the backing to the same size as the quilt top.

3. Beginning in the center and working outward in a sunburst pattern, baste all three layers together using long stitches.

4. Using running stitches, quilt ¼ inch on each side of all seam lines.

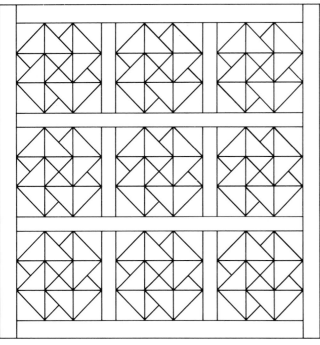

Figure 3

To finish

1. When all quilting has been completed, clip away the basting stitches.

2. Trim the batting ½ inch smaller than the quilt top.

3. Turn the raw edges of the quilt top ¼ inch to the inside and press.

4. Turn the raw edges of the backing ¼ inch to the inside and press.

5. Pin the front and back edges together and slipstitch or machine stitch all around to finish.

To hang

Because this wall hanging is quite light, it is easy to hang without any extra precautions. A Velcro strip can be stitched along the back top edge of the quilt. Stitch through the backing and filling, but not the quilt top. The other side of the Velcro is then stuck to a length of board which is mounted to the wall. Or, you can simply place the other half of the Velcro in position on the wall and mount the hanging directly. I have mounted Susan Joyce's wall hanging in my office with small Velcro tabs that I placed on the backs of all four corners and at equal distances along all four edges. In this way it adheres to the wall and stays perfectly flat.

FAIR AND SQUARE

Because the squares are fairly large and the pattern is simple, this is one of the easiest quilts in the book. Made from solid fabrics, this project would look equally good made with a combination of calico prints. The overall quilting gives it texture and, because the blocks are set on the diagonal, this is an interesting quilt. You can do as much or as little hand quilting as desired. The finished project measures 68 × 68 inches, which fits either a twin or double bed. If you want to enlarge this quilt, simply add another border approximately 8 inches all around and you'll increase the size by an additional 16 inches at the top, bottom, and sides.

BLUE AND WHITE MISSOURI STAR

The many variations of star patterns have always been popular for quiltmaking. Using two shades of blue with white makes this quilt bold and graphic. It was designed and made by Peter Peluso, Jr., a graphic designer who became fascinated with the idea of applying his design and needlework skills to quilt-making. The finished quilt is 73 × 73 inches, which will fit a double or queen-size bed.

3. With right sides facing and raw edges aligned, stitch one of these strips to the top edge of a row. Open seams and press.

4. Repeat with a strip on the bottom edge of the row.

5. Continue to join all 5 rows, separated by the lattice strips, in this way (see Figure 3). Open seams and press.

Borders

1. With right sides facing and raw edges aligned, stitch a 2½ × 69½-inch border strip to the top edge of the quilt top. Open seams and press.

2. Repeat on the bottom edge.

3. Join the 2½ × 73½-inch border strips to the sides of the quilt top in the same way. Open seams and press.

To quilt

1. Cut the backing fabric in half to make 2 pieces, each 2⅛ yards long.

2. With right sides facing and raw edges aligned, stitch the 2 pieces together along one long edge. Open seams and press. Trim to quilt top size.

3. With wrong sides facing and batting in between, pin the backing and quilt top together.

4. Starting at the center and working outward in a sunburst pattern, baste all 3 layers together with long, loose stitches.

5. To hand quilt, take small running stitches through all 3 layers, ¼-inch on both sides of each seam line. *Do not stitch into the ½-inch seam allowance around outer edges.*

6. To machine quilt, stitch along all seam lines.

To finish

1. When all quilting has been completed, remove basting stitches.

2. Turn raw edges of the top under ¼ inch and press.

3. Fold backing edges to the inside ¼ inch and press.

4. Slipstitch or machine stitch all around to finish.

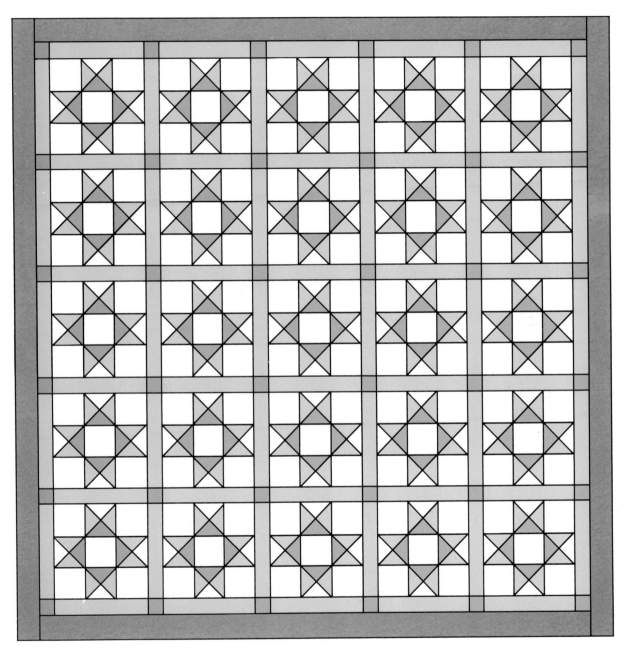

Figure 3

WOOL COVERLET

Although most patchwork quilts are made of cotton or polyester, I thought you might like to make a coverlet of wool scraps for a change. This is a good way to reuse frayed or worn-out, faded flannel shirts, old blankets, jackets, and pants. Patterns and solids work well together. If you don't have scraps on hand, consider buying ¼- or ½-yard pieces of a variety of different wool and flannel pieces. The backing can be made from a solid piece of one of the fabrics, or you can back the pieced top with muslin. The finished size is 49 × 64 inches.

Roman Stripes

This wall hanging is a good example of how to combine color with an interesting pattern. Using various shades of different colors, Susan Fernald Joyce has created a beautiful rendition of this popular early quilt design. The 42-inch square is the perfect size for economical use of 45-inch-wide fabric. The intricate hand quilting around the borders makes this a special quilt. I have this one hanging on my office wall, and it adds warmth and a country feeling to an otherwise businesslike environment.

MAZE OF GRAYS

Avis Skinner has a terrific eye for antique quilts. Stepping into her store, Vis-à-Vis on Main Street, Nantucket Island, is an experience for the most discerning collector. Here one finds exquisite, lace-trimmed bed linens and country rugs as well as clothing and accessories. But it's the early American quilts, piled everywhere, that draw us back over and over again. Almost weekly the front display window featuring an early wrought-iron bed is outfitted with a different quilt, usually befitting the season or special occasion. For every Fourth of July weekend, Avis always manages to find yet another perfect red, white, and blue quilt.

The quilt shown here is distinctive because you don't often find a quilt made with gray and white fabric. This quilt is unusual because it has a country feeling but looks contemporary at the same time. Because it's easy to make, I asked if we might borrow it to include in the book. An ample 70×70 inches, the quilt is basically made of four large blocks that are created by adding strips. The pattern is similar to a Log Cabin design, but easier. When buying fabric, take care to choose an interesting gray print.

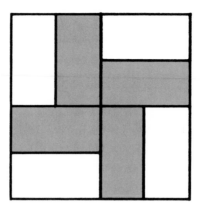

BABY STRIPES

It's easy to make a baby quilt in a weekend. In fact, if you do as I did here and use a striped sheet rather than piecing together strips of fabric, you can make this quilt in a day! The pink-striped fabric is a Laura Ashley sheet, which first should be washed to soften it and to remove the sizing. This makes it easier to quilt. One single sheet is more than enough for the front and back. However, to give this quilt a contrasting backing, I used a thin-striped pink and white fabric. The stripes on the sheet are 2 inches wide, and the overall finished size is 34 × 42 inches.

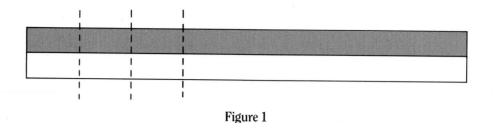

Figure 1

MATERIALS

Note: Even though a single sheet was used to make this quilt, all yardages are figured for fabric 45 inches wide.

¾ yard pink fabric

¾ yard white fabric

1 yard pink pinstripe for the backing

quilt batting

DIRECTIONS

Note: All measurements include a ¼-inch seam allowance.

Cut the following

from pink:

10 strips, each 2½ × 36 inches

from white:

10 strips, each 2½ × 36 inches

Strip piecing

1. With right sides facing and raw edges aligned, stitch a pink strip to a white strip along one long edge. Open seam and press.

2. Cut this pink-and-white strip into 4½-inch segments as shown in Figure 1.

3. Make 80 pink-and-white segments, each 4½ × 4½ inches.

To make a block

1. With right sides facing and raw edges aligned, stitch 4 segments together so that, as shown in Figure 2, the pink strips form a pinwheel in the center of the block.

2. Open seams and press. Make 20 blocks in this way.

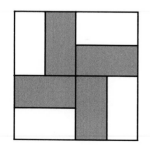

Figure 2

To make a row

1. With right sides facing and raw edges aligned, stitch 2 blocks together along one side. Open seams and press.

2. Continue to join 2 more blocks until you have a row of 4 blocks.

3. Open seams and press. Make 5 rows in this way.

Joining rows

1. With right sides facing and raw edges aligned, stitch Row 1 to Row 2 along the bottom edge. Open seams and press.

2. Continue to join all 5 rows in this way as shown in Figure 3.

To quilt

1. Center the batting on the wrong side of the backing fabric and place the quilt top over the batting, right side up. Pin together.

2. Starting at the center and working outward in a sunburst pattern, baste together with long, loose stitches.

3. Take small running stitches ¼ inch on each side of all seam lines.

To finish

1. When all quilting has been completed, clip away basting stitches.

2. Trim the batting ½ inch smaller than the quilt top all around.

3. Trim the backing so that there is the same amount of extra fabric— approximately 1½ to 2 inches—all around the quilt top.

4. Turn the raw edges of the backing forward ¼ inch and press. Turn the remaining fabric over onto the front of the quilt to create a border. Press and pin all around.

5. Machine or slipstitch the border to the quilt top to finish.

Figure 3

HARLEQUIN SQUARES

This 76 × 76-inch quilt was made to fit a queen-size bed. The pattern is made by piecing squares set on the diagonal, with the blocks separated by wide borders. This is an easy quilt to adapt for a single bed. Simply subtract a row of blocks in each direction and adjust the size of the borders accordingly.

The orange, blue, and yellow calico prints are typical of country quilts, but you can change the color combination to suit your decorating needs. You might like to use a print and a solid in light and dark contrasting colors with a printed border all around. Almost any colors will look good in this design.

MATERIALS

Note: Yardages are figured for fabric 45 inches wide.

3 yards white fabric (bleached muslin is nice for this project)

5¼ yards pink fabric (includes 3½ yards for backing)

quilt batting

tracing paper

water-soluble quilt marker

DIRECTIONS

Note: All measurements include a ¼-inch seam allowance.

Cut the following

from white:

        borders —

        2 strips, each 4½ × 70½ inches

        2 strips, each 4½ × 53½ inches

     15 squares, each 9½ × 9½ inches

     60 squares, each 3½ × 3½ inches

     60 squares, each 3⅛ × 3⅛ inches; cut each square into

        2 triangles (120 triangles)

     4 squares, each 4½ × 4½ inches

from pink:

        borders—

        2 strips, 4½ × 54½ inches

        2 strips, 4½ × 45½ inches

     15 squares, each 3½ × 3½ inches

     60 squares, each 3⅛ × 3⅛ inches; cut each square into

        2 triangles (120 triangles)

To make a square

1. With right sides facing and raw edges aligned, stitch a pink triangle to a white triangle to make a larger triangle. Open seam and press. Make 2.

2. Next, stitch these 2 pink and white triangles together to make a square as shown in Figure 1.

3. Open seam and press. Make 4 squares in this way.

Figure 1

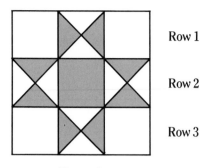

Row 1

Row 2

Row 3

Figure 2

To make a block

Refer to Figure 2.

1. With right sides facing and raw edges aligned, stitch a white square to a pink-and-white triangle square along the right side. Open seams and press.

2. With right sides facing and raw edges aligned, add a white square to make a row. Open seam and press.

3. Next, stitch a pink-and-white triangle square to a pink square, followed by another triangle square, to make a row as shown in Figure 2. Open seams and press.

4. Repeat Row 1 to make Row 3 of the block.

5. With right sides facing and raw edges aligned, join Row 1 and Row 2. Open seam and press.

6. Next, join Row 3 to make a block. Open seam and press. Make 15 blocks in this way.

To make a row

Refer to Figure 3.

Row 1

1. With right sides facing and raw edges aligned, stitch a block to a large white square along the right side. Open seam and press.

2. Continue with another block, then a white square, ending with another block. Open seams and press. Make 3 rows in this way.

Row 2

1. With right sides facing and raw edges aligned, stitch a white square to a block along the right side. Open seams and press.

2. Continue by adding a white square, another block, then a white square to complete the row. Open seams and press. Make 3 rows in this way.

Joining rows

1. With right sides facing and raw edges aligned, join Row 1 to Row 2 along one long edge. Open seam and press.

2. Continue to join rows, alternating Rows 1 and 2 as shown in Figure 3. Open seams and press.

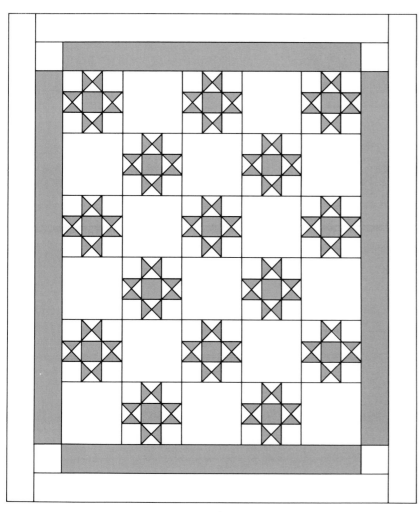

Figure 3

Borders

1. With right sides facing and raw edges aligned, stitch a $4\frac{1}{2} \times 45\frac{1}{2}$-inch pink border strip to the top edge of the quilt top. Open seam and press.

2. Join the bottom border strip in the same way.

3. Next, stitch a white $4\frac{1}{2} \times 4\frac{1}{2}$-inch square to each end of the $4\frac{1}{2} \times 54\frac{1}{2}$-inch pink border strips. Open seams and press.

4. With right sides facing and raw edges aligned, stitch these pieces to each side edge of the quilt top. Open seams and press.

5. With right sides facing and raw edges aligned, join a white $4\frac{1}{2} \times 53\frac{1}{2}$-inch border strip to the top edge of the quilt top. Open seam and press.

6. Repeat on the bottom edge.

7. Next, join the white $4\frac{1}{2} \times 70\frac{1}{2}$-inch side border strips to each side edge of the quilt top. Open seams and press.

To quilt

1. Using a ruler and a quilt marker, draw a grid on the diagonal over the border areas to be quilted. (See page 12 for details.)

2. The large white squares are quilted in a spider web pattern. The pattern shown here is $\frac{1}{4}$ of the design. Trace the pattern and transfer it to the corner of each white square so that the design meets in the center and fills the square, forming a spider web. (See page 13 for transferring details.)

3. Cut the remaining pink fabric in half and stitch the 2 pieces together along the long edge to create the backing piece.

4. Center the quilt batting on the wrong side of the backing. With right side facing up, center the quilt top over the batting so there is equal backing fabric all around. Pin all 3 layers together.

5. Starting at the center and working outward in a sunburst pattern, baste the fabrics together with long, loose stitches.

6. Take small running stitches along all premarked quilt lines. (See page 15 for quilting details.)

To finish

1. Remove all basting stitches.

2. Trim the batting to the same size as the quilt top.

3. Trim the backing to 1 inch larger than the quilt top all around.

4. Turn the raw edge of the backing forward $\frac{1}{2}$ inch and press.

5. Fold the remaining $\frac{1}{2}$ inch over onto the quilt top to create a $\frac{1}{2}$-inch pink border all around. Slipstitch or machine stitch to finish.

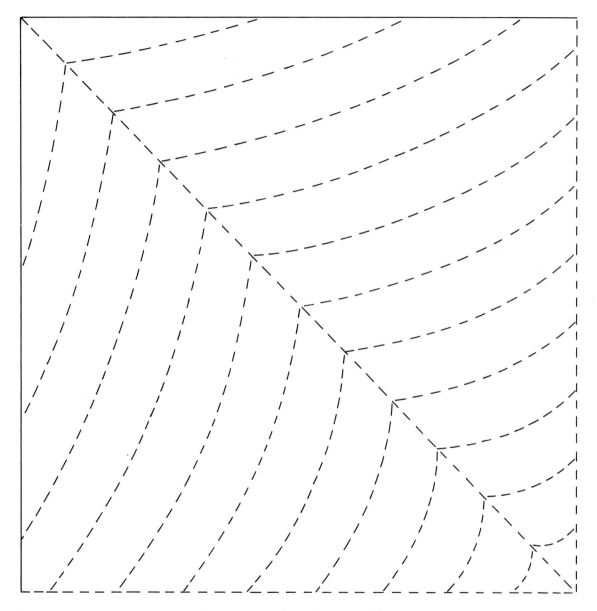

LeMoyne Star quilting pattern—¼ of design

BABY BLOCKS

Gingham fabric is delightful for use in a baby quilt. It comes in a variety of pastel colors and in checks of different sizes. I prefer the small checked gingham for this project, which was designed and made by my daughter Robby, who is our studio manager. The combination of blue, green, and white is perfect for a shower gift when you don't know if the baby will be a boy or a girl. The pattern, known as Around the World, is often used to make wall hangings. The finished size is 42 × 42 inches.

MATERIALS

Note: Yardages are figured for fabric 45 inches wide.

½ yard green gingham (A)

¾ yard white fabric (B)

1 yard blue gingham (C)

1¼ yards backing fabric (can be one of the fabrics above)

quilt batting

water-soluble fabric marker

tracing paper

DIRECTIONS

Note: All measurements include a ¼-inch seam allowance.

Cut the following

from green (A):

    20 squares, each 3½ × 3½ inches

    4 strips, each 3½ × 15½ inches

from white (B):

    2 strips, each 2 × 36½ inches

    2 strips, each 2 × 33½ inches

    37 squares, each 3½ × 3½ inches

from blue (C):

    2 strips, each 3½ × 42½ inches

    2 strips, each 3½ × 36½ inches

    4 rectangles, each 3½ × 9½ inches

    4 rectangles, each 3½ × 6½ inches

    24 squares, each 3½ × 3½ inches

1. With right sides facing and raw edges aligned, stitch a green A square to another green A square along one side edge. Open seam and press.

2. Continue to join squares in this way, following the sequence below. You will have 9 rows of 9 squares each.

    Row 1: A-A-C-B-B-B-C-A-A

    Row 2: A-C-B-B-C-B-B-C-A

    Row 3: C-B-B-C-A-C-B-B-C

Row 4: B-B-C-A-B-A-C-B-B

Row 5: B-C-A-B-B-B-A-C-B

Row 6: B-B-C-A-B-A-C-B-B

Row 7: C-B-B-C-A-C-B-B-C

Row 8: A-C-B-B-C-B-B-C-A

Row 9: A-A-C-B-B-B-C-A-A

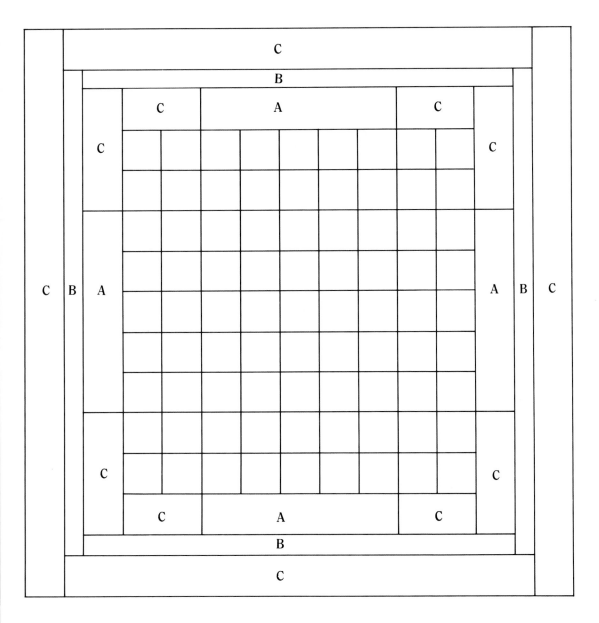

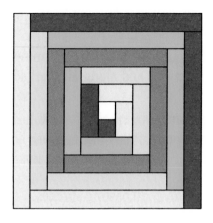

LOG CABIN
WALL HANGING

This beautiful example of a Log Cabin wall hanging was designed by fiber artist Deborah Odell. She chose to combine dark and light calico prints, using shades of green offset by light grays as the dominant color scheme. The finished size is 40×40 inches. This is the perfect way to add interest to any area of your home.

MATERIALS

Note: Yardages are figured for fabric 45 inches wide.

piece of pink calico scrap

a variety of gray calico scraps

a variety of green calico scraps

½ yard dark-blue or black calico for the border strips

1¼ yards backing fabric

quilt batting

Velcro tabs for hanging

DIRECTIONS

Note: All measurements include a ¼-inch seam allowance.

Cut the following

from pink (A):

4 squares, each 1½ × 1½ inches

from light-gray calicos:

4 squares, each 1½ × 1½ inches (B)
4 strips, each 1½ × 2½ inches (C)
4 strips, each 1½ × 3½ inches (F)
4 strips, each 1½ × 4½ inches (G)
4 strips, each 1½ × 5½ inches (J)
4 strips, each 1½ × 6½ inches (K)
4 strips, each 1½ × 7½ inches (N)
4 strips, each 1½ × 8½ inches (O)
4 strips, each 1½ × 9½ inches (R)
4 strips, each 1½ × 10½ inches (S)

from green calicos:

4 strips, each 1½ × 2½ inches (D)
4 strips, each 1½ × 3½ inches (E)
4 strips, each 1½ × 4½ inches (H)
4 strips, each 1½ × 5½ inches (I)
4 strips, each 1½ × 6½ inches (L)
4 strips, each 1½ × 7½ inches (M)
4 strips, each 1½ × 8½ inches (P)
4 strips, each 1½ × 9½ inches (Q)
4 strips, each 1½ × 10½ inches (T)
4 strips, each 1½ × 11½ inches (U)

from green or gray calicos:

        inside borders—
        2 strips, each 1½ × 22½ inches (V)
        4 strips, each 1½ × 24½ inches (W)
        4 strips, each 1½ × 46½ inches (X)
        4 strips, each 1½ × 28½ inches (Y)
        4 strips, each 1½ × 30½ inches (Z)
        2 strips, each 1½ × 32½ inches (AA)

from dark calico:

        outside borders—
        2 strips, each 4½ × 32½ inches
        2 strips, each 4½ × 40½ inches

To make a block

Refer to Figure 1.

1. With right sides facing and raw edges aligned, stitch an A square to a B square. Open seams and press.

2. With right sides facing and raw edges aligned, join this unit to one long side of a C strip as shown. This is the center of the block.

3. Continue to add strips D through U as shown in Figure 2. This completes the block. Open seams and press. Make 4 blocks.

To join blocks

Refer to Figure 3.

1. With right sides facing and raw edges aligned, join 2 blocks, with the gray areas meeting in the lower center, and stitch along the right, side edge. Open seams and press.

2. Repeat with the remaining 2 blocks so that the gray areas are at the top center of the joined blocks. Open seams and press.

3. With right sides facing and raw edges aligned, join the 4 blocks so that the gray areas come together in the center. Open seams and press.

Inside borders

Refer to Figure 4.

1. With right sides facing and raw edges aligned, stitch a V strip to one side edge of the quilt top. Open seam and press.

2. Repeat on the opposite side.

Figure 1

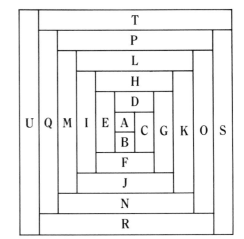

Figure 2

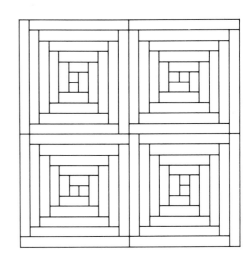

Figure 3

79

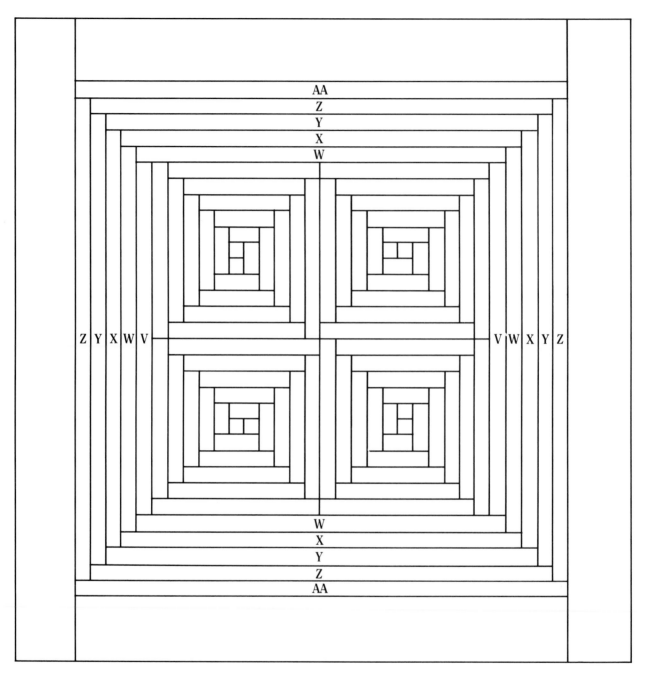

Figure 4

3. Next, join 2 W strips to the top and bottom of the quilt top.

4. Join the remaining W strips to the sides of the quilt top.

5. Continue in this way with strips X through AA as shown in Figure 4.

6. Open all seams and press.

Outside borders

1. With right sides facing and raw edges aligned, join the $4\frac{1}{2} \times 32\frac{1}{2}$-inch border strips to the top and bottom of the quilt top. Open seams and press.

2. Next, join the $4\frac{1}{2} \times 40\frac{1}{2}$-inch border strips to the sides of the quilt top. Open seams and press.

To quilt

1. With wrong sides of the fabric facing, pin the top, batting, and backing together.

2. Beginning in the center and working outward in a sunburst pattern, baste all 3 layers together with long stitches.

3. Using small running stitches, quilt $\frac{1}{8}$ inch on each side of all seam lines. Do not quilt into outside seam allowance.

To finish

1. Remove all basting stitches.

2. Trim the batting $\frac{1}{2}$ inch smaller than the quilt top all around.

3. Trim the backing fabric to same size as the quilt top.

4. Turn the raw edges of the quilt top and the backing $\frac{1}{4}$ inch to the inside and press. Pin together.

5. Slipstitch or machine stitch all around to finish.

To hang

Place a Velcro tab at the back of each corner of the quilt with corresponding tabs on the wall where the quilt will hang. (For other methods of hanging a quilt, see page 17.)

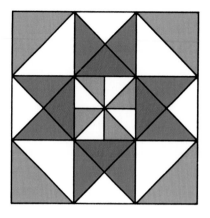

PINWHEEL STAR

Star patterns are the most popular among quilt designs, and there are an endless number of variations. The combination of red, white, and blue fabric always looks good, and combining solids and calicos makes the quilt pattern all the more interesting. This quilt is made up of 20 blocks, and the finished project measures 77 × 95 inches, large enough to fit a double or queen-size bed.

MATERIALS

Note: Yardages are figured for fabric 45 inches wide.

2¾ yards blue print

2¾ yards white fabric

5 yards solid-blue fabric to match print (backing and border fabric)

quilt batting

DIRECTIONS

Note: All measurements include a ¼-inch seam allowance.

Cut the following

from blue print:

    1 piece 30 × 58 inches

    14 strips, each 3½ × 42½ inches

from white:

    1 piece 30 × 58 inches

    14 strips, each 3½ × 42½ inches

from solid blue:

    Cut the fabric in half so you have 2 pieces, each 2½ yards. Use one piece to cut your borders.

        borders —

        2 strips, each 3½ × 84½ inches

        2 strips, each 3½ × 66½ inches

Quick-and-easy triangle method

Refer to Figure 1.

1. On the back of the white 30 × 58-inch fabric, measure and mark 32 squares, each 7 × 7 inches, so you have 4 across and 8 down (Figure 1a).

2. Next, draw a diagonal line through all the squares.

3. With right sides facing, pin to the same-size blue print fabric.

4. Stitch ¼ inch on each side of all diagonal lines.

5. Cut on all solid drawn lines. You will have 64 squares made of blue print and white triangles. This is Unit 1 (see Figure 1b).

6. Open all seams and press.

Figure 1

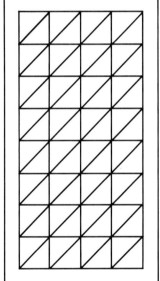

1a Cutting diagram for quick-and-easy triangle method

1b Unit 1

MATERIALS

Note: Yardages are figured for fabric 45 inches wide.

½ yard rose fabric (A)

½ yard light-green fabric (B)

½ yard dark-green fabric (C)

1 yard light-brown fabric (D)

2¼ yards mustard fabric (E)

3¾ yards backing fabric

thin quilt batting

for wall hanging: canvas stretcher approximately ½ to 1 inch
    larger than finished quilt

borders (optional): 2 strips 2 × 66½ inches and 2 strips
    2 × 84½ inches

water-soluble quilting marker

tracing paper

DIRECTIONS

Note: All measurements include a ¼-inch seam allowance.

Cut the following

from rose (A):
    30 squares, each 3½ × 3½ inches

from light green (B):
    60 squares, each 3½ × 3½ inches

from dark green (C):
    60 squares, each 3½ × 3½ inches

from light brown (D):
    120 squares, each 3½ × 3½ inches

from mustard (E):
    4 lattice strips 5½ × 79½ inches
    25 lattice strips 5½ × 9½ inches

To make a block

Refer to Figure 1.

1. With right sides facing and raw edges aligned, stitch a light-brown D square to a dark-green C square along one side edge. Open seam and press.

D	C	D
B	A	B
D	C	D

Figure 1

97

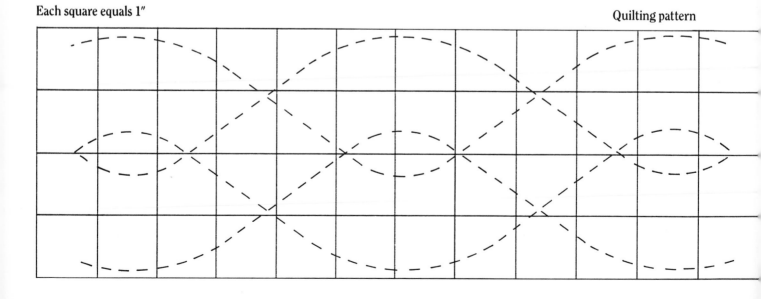

Figure 2

2. Next, join another light-brown D square to the opposite side of the green C square to make a row of 3 squares. Open seam and press.

3. With right sides facing and raw edges aligned, join a green B square to a rose A square followed by a green B square for the center row of the block as shown in Figure 1.

4. Repeat step 1 for the third row of the block. Open seams and press.

5. With right sides facing and raw edges aligned, stitch Rows 1 and 2 together along the long edge. Open seams and press.

6. Join Row 3 to Row 2 in the same way. Make 30 blocks.

To make a row

Refer to Figure 2.

1. With right sides facing and raw edges aligned, join a block to one 5½ × 9½-inch lattice strip along the right edge. Open seam and press.

2. Continue to join blocks separated by lattice strips in this way. You will have a row of 6 blocks and 5 lattice strips. Open seams and press. Make 5 rows.

To join rows

1. With right sides facing and raw edges aligned, join Row 1 to 5½ × 79½-inch mustard lattice strip. Open seam and press.

2. Continue to join rows separated by lattice strips in this way.

3. Open seams and press.

Each square equals 1″

Quilting pattern

For framing

If you wish to hang this quilt, you'll need to add a 2-inch border all around to stretch over the canvas frame. For the border fabrics you can use either one of the colors in the wall hanging or a contrasting fabric.

1. With right sides facing and raw edges aligned, join the top and bottom borders to the top and bottom edges of the quilt top. Open seams and press.

2. Repeat with the side border strips.

To quilt

1. Trace the quilting design and transfer to the lattice strips on the quilt top (see page 15 for quilting details).

2. Cut the backing fabric in half and stitch these 2 pieces together along the long edge. Open seams and press.

3. Trim the backing and batting to the same size as the quilt top (excluding the border).

4. Starting in the center and moving outward in a sunburst pattern, baste the backing, batting, and top together with long stitches through all 3 layers.

5. Take small running stitches about ¼ inch on each side of all seam lines and along all premarked quilting lines. Do not quilt into the seam allowance all around the outside edge of the quilt.

To finish

1. When quilting has been completed, clip away basting stitches.

2. If you are making this project as a quilt and not as a wall hanging, trim the batting ¼ inch smaller than the quilt top all around.

3. Turn the raw edges of the quilt top ¼ inch to the inside and press. Turn the backing fabric in ¼ inch and press.

4. Slipstitch or machine stitch all around to finish.

5. *If framing:* Place the quilted hanging facedown on a flat, hard surface and center the stretcher frame on top. Pull the excess border fabric evenly taut to the back of the frame and staple it all around.

6. If you want to hang the quilt without stretching it over a frame, simply attach Velcro along the top and bottom edges of the back of the quilt, add corresponding strips to the wall, and attach (see page 17).

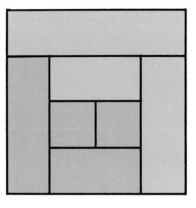

BARN RAISING

SSusan Fernald Joyce's wall hanging is a beautiful version of the traditional Barn Raising pattern. Contrasting solid fabrics in shades of purple, blue, pink, and green with black make this a very dramatic quilt. Because the finished quilt is a 44-inch square, the full 45-inch width of one piece of fabric can be used for the backing.

MATERIALS

Note: Yardages are figured for fabric 45 inches wide.

light-color fabric:

    ¼ yard aqua

    ½ yard lavender

    ¼ yard light gray

    ¼ yard pink

dark-color fabric:

    ¼ yard green

    ¼ yard rose

    ¼ yard dark gray

    ¾ yard black

    1½ yards purple (includes backing)

thin quilt batting

tracing paper

water-soluble quilt marker

DIRECTIONS

Note: All measurements include a ¼-inch seam allowance.

Cut the following

from pink:

    borders—

    2 strips, each $2 \times 39\frac{1}{2}$ inches

    2 strips, each $2 \times 36\frac{1}{2}$ inches

from lavender:

    borders—

    2 strips, each $3 \times 44\frac{1}{2}$ inches

    2 strips, each $3 \times 39\frac{1}{2}$ inches

from each of the light colors (including pink and lavender):

    9 squares, each 2×2 inches (A)

    9 pieces, each 2×5 inches (E)

from purple:

    backing piece, 45×45 inches

from each of the dark colors (including purple):

    9 pieces, each 2 × 3½ inches (C)
    9 pieces, each 2 × 6½ inches (G)

from black:

    36 squares, each 2 × 2 inches (B)
    36 pieces, each 2 × 3½ inches (D)
    36 pieces, each 2 × 5 inches (F)

Note: Within a block, use the same light color for pieces A and E and the same dark color for pieces C and G.

To make Block 1

Refer to Figure 1.

1. With right sides facing and raw edges aligned, join an A piece to a B piece. Open seam and press.

2. Next, join a C piece to the long left side of the A/B piece as shown in the diagram.

3. Continue by joining a D piece to the right side of the A/B piece in the same way.

4. Using the same light color as you did for the A piece, join an E piece to the top edge of the pieced square, followed by an F piece to the bottom edge.

5. Finish with a G piece on the left, side edge. Open seams and press.

6. Make 14 of Block 1.

To make Block 2

Refer to Figure 2.

1. With right sides facing and raw edges aligned, join a B piece to the left side edge of an A piece. Open seam and press.

2. Next, stitch a C piece to the long bottom edge and a D piece to the long top edge.

3. With right sides facing and raw edges aligned, stitch an E piece to the long right edge and an F piece to the long left edge.

4. Join a G piece along the bottom long edge in the same way, open seam, and press.

5. Make 22 of Block 2.

Figure 1

Block 1

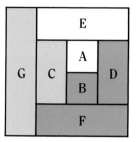

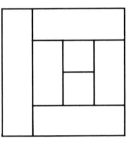

Figure 2

Block 2

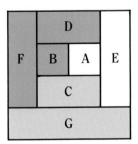

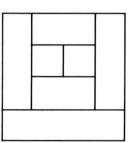

To join blocks

Refer to Figure 3.

1. With right sides facing and raw edges aligned, stitch Block 1 to Block 2 as shown in Figure 3.

2. Continue to join another Block 1, then a Block 2, followed by 2 more of Block 1 as shown, to make a row of 6 blocks.

3. Continue to join blocks, as shown, to make a total of 6 rows.

Figure 3

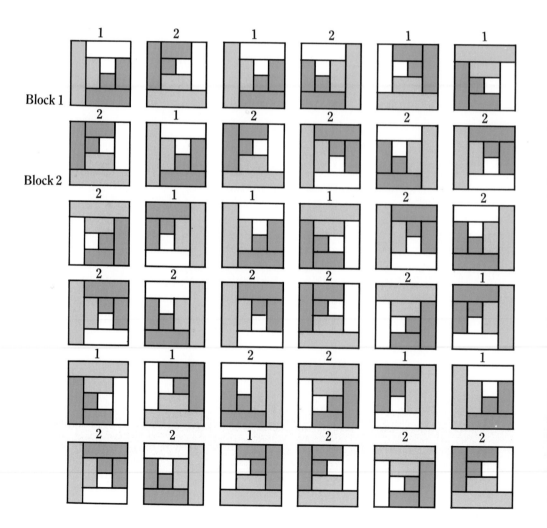

Joining rows

1. With right sides facing and raw edges aligned, join Row 1 to the top edge of Row 2. Open seam and press.

2. Continue to join all 6 rows in this way.

Borders

1. With right sides facing and raw edges aligned, stitch a $2 \times 36\frac{1}{2}$-inch pink border strip to the top edge of the quilt top. Open seam and press.

2. Repeat on the bottom edge.

3. Next, join the $2 \times 39\frac{1}{2}$-inch pink border strips to each side of the quilt top. Open seams and press.

4. With right sides facing and raw edges aligned, stitch a $3 \times 39\frac{1}{2}$-inch lavender border to the top edge of the quilt top. Open seam and press.

5. Repeat on the bottom edge.

6. Join the remaining lavender border strips to each side of the quilt as shown in Figure 4.

To quilt

1. Transfer the quilting pattern to the border of the quilt. (See page 13.)

2. Use a ruler and a marking pen to draw evenly spaced diagonal lines to form a diamond pattern on the quilt top. (See page 12.)

3. Cut the batting to the same size as the quilt top.

4. Center the batting on the wrong side of the backing. The backing is slightly larger than the quilt top all around.

5. With right sides up, pin the top to the batting and the backing.

6. Starting at the center and working outward in a sunburst pattern, baste the 3 layers together with long, loose stitches.

7. Follow all premarked quilting lines and take small running stitches to quilt. (See page 15 for quilting details.)

To finish

1. Remove all basting stitches.

2. Fold the raw edges of the backing fabric forward ¼ inch and press.

3. Bring the folded edge forward to cover the raw edges of the quilt top and press.

4. Slipstitch or machine stitch all around to finish.

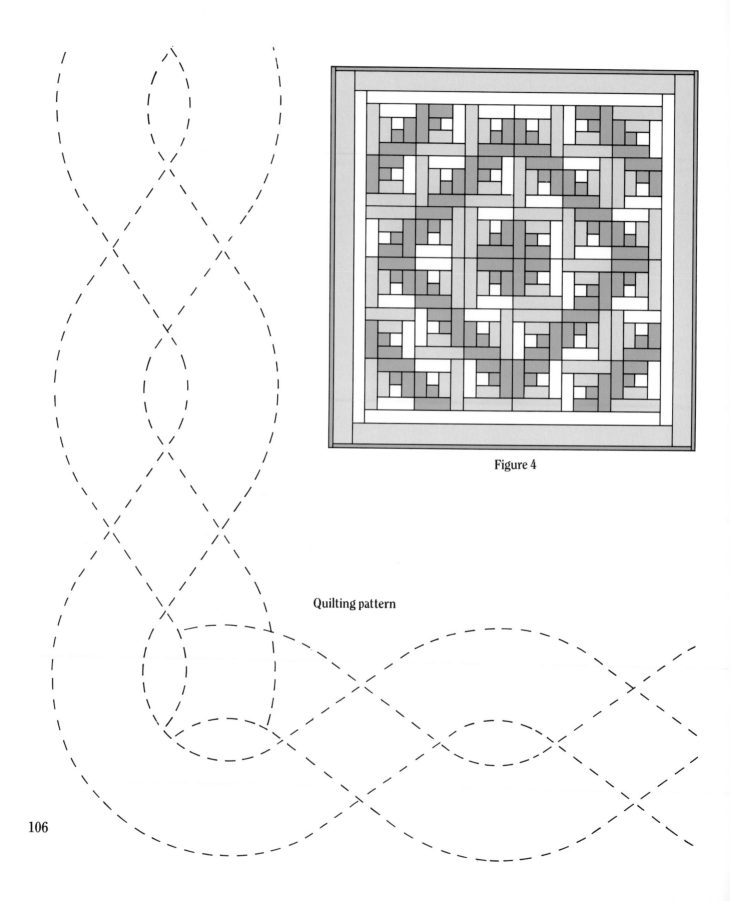

Figure 4

Quilting pattern

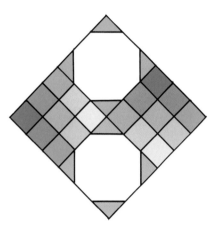

WEDDING WREATH

This quilt would make the perfect wedding gift. It's a little different from the traditional wedding-ring design and is particularly pretty because of the rich color combination. Although the blocks look circular, they are made from squares and right triangles. The quilting design in each of the white squares is called a lover's knot. The finished quilt is approximately 64 × 89 inches.

MATERIALS

Note: Yardages are figured for fabric 45 inches wide.

3 yards total of an assortment of pinks, greens, blues, browns

1 yard tan fabric

2½ yards white fabric

3¾ yards backing fabric

quilt batting

tracing paper

water-soluble quilt marker

stiff paper for template (see pages 11 and 18)

DIRECTIONS

Note: All measurements include a ¼-inch seam allowance.

Cut the following

from the assortment of colors:

     70 squares, each 4 × 4 inches; cut each square into 2
          triangles (140 triangles)

     216 squares, each 3½ × 3½ inches

from tan:

     10 squares, each 10 × 10 inches; cut each square into 2
          triangles (20 triangles)

     1 square 10½ × 10½ inches; cut into 4 triangles

from white:

     35 from the template piece shown in the art

To make Block A

Refer to Figure 1.

1. With right sides facing and raw edges aligned, stitch 4 of the small triangles to each corner of a white template piece as shown in the diagram.

2. Open seams and press. Make 35 blocks in this way.

To make Block B

Refer to Figure 2.

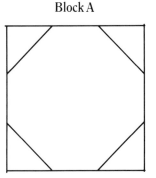

Figure 1

Block A

MATERIALS

Note: Yardages are figured for fabric 45 inches wide.

A total of 4 yards of assorted light cotton fabrics (scrap pieces should be 6 × 6 inches each)

2¼ yards bleached muslin for borders (muslin can be 36 inches wide)

4½ yards backing fabric (if muslin, use fabric 45 inches wide)
quilt batting
water-soluble quilt marker

DIRECTIONS

Note: All measurements include a ¼-inch seam allowance.

Cut the following

from a variety of cottons:

     144 squares, each 6 × 6 inches

from muslin:

       borders—
       2 strips, each 6 × 66½ inches
       2 strips, each 6 × 77½ inches

To make a row

1. Plan and lay out your squares so that you have 12 rows of 12 squares each, with the fabrics alternating in an interesting pattern. Keep moving the squares around until you are satisfied with the arrangement.

2. With right sides facing and raw edges aligned, stitch 2 squares together along one side edge.

3. Open seams and press unless you are using worn fabric that is quite thin. In this case, instead of opening the seams, press them to one side to give the quilt more strength.

4. Continue to join 10 more squares in this way, making a horizontal row of 12 squares.

5. Make 12 rows of 12 squares each.

Joining rows

1. With right sides facing and raw edges aligned, stitch 2 rows together, making sure to match all seams.

2. Press.

3. Continue to join all 12 rows in this way.

Borders

1. With right sides facing and raw edges aligned, stitch a 6 × 66½-inch border strip to the top edge of the quilt.

2. Press.

3. Next, join the bottom border strip in the same way.

4. With right sides facing and raw edges aligned, join the remaining strips to each side. Press.

To quilt

1. Since each square is large, this quilt will look best with an overall grid pattern of quilting stitches. (See page 12 for complete marking directions.) However, for a quicker quilting project, you can run your quilting stitches on each side of all seam lines. This way you won't need any marking lines to follow.

2. Cut the backing fabric in half. Join the 2 pieces lengthwise. Open seams and press.

3. With wrong sides facing and the batting in between, pin the backing and pieced top together.

4. Starting in the center and working outward in a sunburst pattern, baste with long, loose stitches.

5. Following the marked grid lines, take small, running stitches through all 3 layers of fabric to quilt. (See page 15 for quilting details.) Or, you can take small running stitches ¼ inch on each side of all seam lines. *Stop quilting stitches ½ inch from the edge of the quilt all around.*

To finish

1. Clip away all basting stitches.

2. Trim the batting all around so that it is ½ inch smaller than the quilt top.

3. Trim the backing so it is ½ inch larger all around than the quilt top.

4. Turn the backing edge forward ¼ inch and press. Turn the remaining ¼ inch over the raw edge of the quilt top and press. Pin all around.

5. Slipstitch or machine stitch the edge to finish.

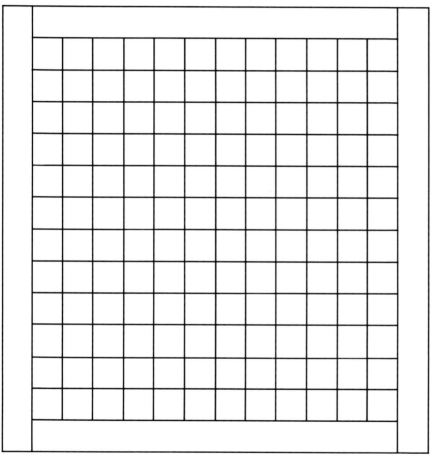

White on White

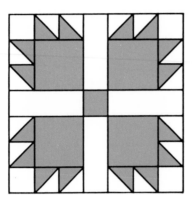

BEAR CLAW

This is a traditional American quilt pattern. The names given to quilts were often taken from everyday objects common to the times or area. The origin of this quilt is quite obvious. The pattern looks best when done in one color with white. For the best-looking results, select a printed calico such as the red shown here, or blue. This quilt, which measures 63 × 63 inches, is made up of 9 blocks.

2. Draw a

3. With rig
white fabric

4. Stitch ¼

5. Cut on a

To make bla

Refer to Figu

1. With righ
to a red/whit

2. Next, joir

3. With rig
squares as sh

4. With righ
squares to or

5. Join Row
2. Open sean

To make a bl

Refer to Figu

1. With righ
(2½ × 6½ in
and press.

2. Next, join
the positionir

3. Repeat by
white rectang

4. With right
inch square t
seam and pres

5. Attach a r
square to mak

6. With right
together to cr
Make 9 blocks

To make a row

1. With right sides facing and raw edges aligned, join a block and a white 5½ × 14½-inch lattice strip along the right side. Open seam and press.

2. Continue to add another block, then a lattice strip, followed by a third block as shown in Figure 4.

3. Open seams and press. Make 3 rows.

Joining rows

Refer to Figure 4.

1. With right sides facing and raw edges aligned, stitch a white 5½ × 52½-inch-long strip to the bottom edge of Row 1. Open seam and press.

2. Continue to join the next row of blocks, then a lattice strip, ending with a final row of blocks as shown in Figure 4.

Figure 4

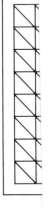

Figure 1
easy tria

Borders

1. With right sides facing and raw edges aligned, stitch a white 5½ × 52½-inch strip to the top edge of the quilt top. Open seam and press.

2. Repeat on the bottom edge of the quilt.

3. With right sides facing and raw edges aligned, join the white 5½ × 62½-inch strips to the sides of the quilt.

4. With right sides facing and raw edges aligned, stitch a red 1 × 62½-inch strip to the top edge of the quilt top. Open seam and press.

5. Repeat on the bottom edge with the same-size red strip.

6. Next, join the red 1 × 63½-inch strips to the sides in the same way. Open seams and press.

To quilt

1. Cut the backing fabric in half and stitch the 2 halves together lengthwise.

2. Using a yardstick and a marker, draw evenly-spaced diagonal lines across the quilt top in both directions including all borders and lattice strips. (See page 12 for marking a quilting grid.)

3. Pin the top, batting, and backing together.

4. Beginning in the center and working outward in a sunburst pattern, use long stitches to baste the top, batting, and backing together through all 3 layers.

5. Using small running stitches, quilt ¼ inch on each side of all seam lines and along all premarked quilting lines.

To finish

1. When all quilting has been completed, clip away the basting stitches.

2. Trim the batting ½ inch smaller than the quilt top.

3. Trim the backing so it is ½ inch larger than the quilt top all around.

4. Turn the raw edges of the top ¼ inch to the inside and press.

5. Turn the raw edges of the backing forward ¼ inch and press. Fold the remaining ¼ inch over onto the front of the quilt, creating a ¼-inch red-print border all around. Press and pin in place.

6. Slipstitch all around to finish.

SUMMER COVERLET

While searching for new ideas in my local fabric shop, I discovered that linen dish toweling can be purchased by the yard. The pretty plaid fabric comes in pale blue, faded red, light aqua, and yellow with white. It is only 18 inches wide, and the bold stripes run down each edge.

After some experimenting with projects, I found that this fabric can be used to make delightful country-style pillows, tablecloths, place mats, and napkins. I cut up squares of the red and blue to make a light and airy country patchwork throw, which also can be used as a table cover if you prefer. This is an easy project because the squares are quite large and the plaid pattern provides lines on which to cut each square. The finished size is 42×56 inches, and each square is 7×7 inches.

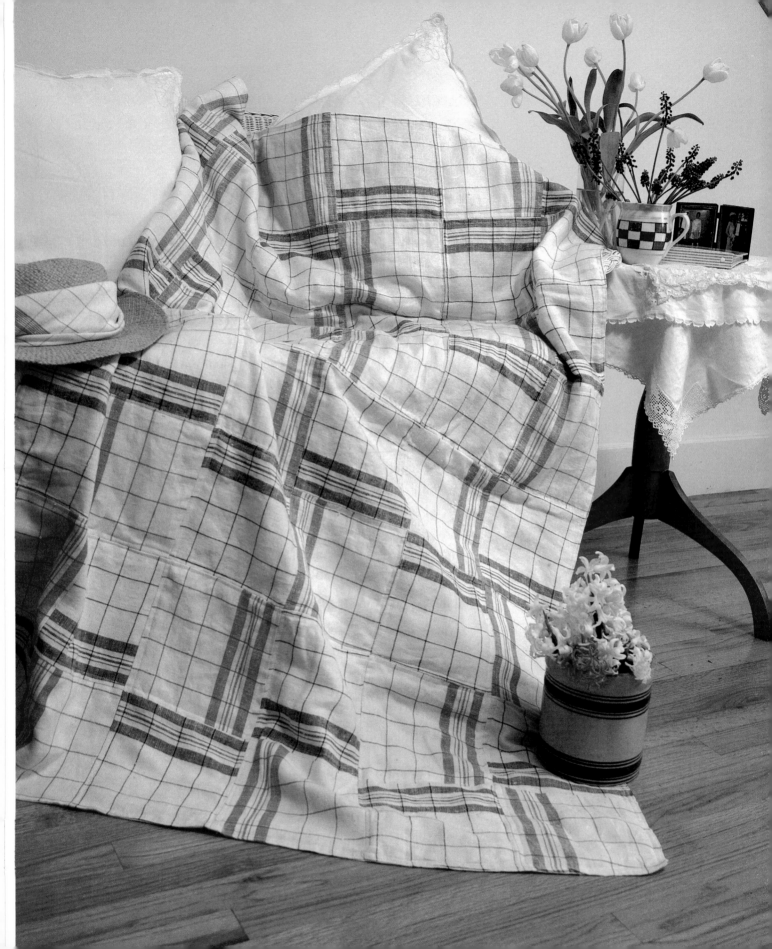

MATERIALS

Note: Yardages are figured for fabric 45 inches wide.

scraps of dark-purple and blue calicos

scraps of light-yellow and tan calicos

¼ yard purple calico or solid fabric for borders

¾ yard backing fabric

thin quilt batting

Velcro tabs for hanging

DIRECTIONS

Note: All measurements include a ¼-inch seam allowance.

Cut the following

from light fabrics:

    A — 8 squares, each 1¼ × 1¼ inches

    D — 8 strips, each 1¼ × 2 inches

    E — 8 strips, each 1¼ × 2¾ inches

    H — 8 strips, each 1¼ × 3½ inches

    I — 8 strips, each 1¼ × 4¼ inches

    L — 8 strips, each 1¼ × 5 inches

    M— 8 strips, each 1¼ × 5¾ inches

    P — 8 strips, each 1¼ × 6½ inches

    Q — 8 strips, each 1¼ × 7¼ inches

    T — 8 strips, each 1¼ × 8 inches

    U — 8 strips, each 1¼ × 8¾ inches

from dark fabrics:

    B — 8 squares, each 1¼ × 1¼ inches

    C — 8 strips, each 1¼ × 2 inches

    F — 8 strips, each 1¼ × 2¾ inches

    G — 8 strips, each 1¼ × 3½ inches

    J — 8 strips, each 1¼ × 4¼ inches

    K — 8 strips, each 1¼ × 5 inches

    N — 8 strips, each 1¼ × 5¾ inches

    O — 8 strips, each 1¼ × 6½ inches

    R — 8 strips, each 1¼ × 7¼ inches

    S — 8 strips, each 1¼ × 8 inches

from purple calico:

    borders—

    2 strips, each 1¼ × 33½ inches (sides)

    4 strips, each 2½ × 20½ inches (top and bottom)

from quilt batting:

    2 strips, each 2¼ × 20¼ inches

    1 piece 18 × 33 inches

To make a block

1. With right sides facing and raw edges aligned, stitch a B square to the top edge of an A square as shown in Figure 1. Open seam and press.

2. With right sides facing and raw edges aligned, join a C strip to the left side of the A/B strip as shown in Figure 1. Open seam and press.

3. With right sides facing and raw edges aligned, build the square and make a block by adding each strip from D through U in sequence according to Figure 2.

4. Open seams and press. Make 8 blocks.

To join blocks

1. Matching the light half of each block, with right sides facing and raw edges aligned, stitch 2 blocks together. Open seam and press.

2. Make 4 rows of 2 blocks each as shown in Figure 3.

3. Open seams and press.

Joining rows

1. With right sides facing and raw edges aligned, stitch Row 1 to Row 2.

2. Open seams and press.

3. Continue to join all 4 rows in this way.

Borders

1. With right sides facing and raw edges aligned, stitch a 1¼ × 33½-inch border strip to each side edge. Open seams and press.

2. With right sides facing and raw edges aligned, pin 2 strips, each 2½ × 20½ inches together. Repeat with the other 2 strips. Cut off the ends of each pinned set at a 45-degree angle. These are the top and bottom borders that frame the quilt.

Figure 1

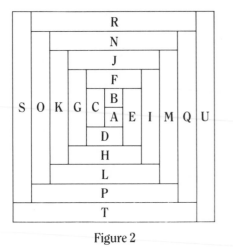

Figure 2

3. Leaving the long edge open on each set of top and bottom border strips, stitch around 3 sides and 4 corners. Turn right side out and press.

4. Cut off the ends of each $2\frac{1}{4} \times 20\frac{1}{4}$-inch batting strip at a 45-degree angle and insert one into each set of top and bottom border strips. Set aside.

To quilt

1. With right sides facing and raw edges aligned, pin the backing and quilt top together.

2. Stitch around 3 sides and 4 corners, leaving one short end open for turning.

3. Trim the seam allowance, clip corners, and turn right side out. Press and insert the piece of batting that is cut a little smaller than the quilt top. If it doesn't lie flat inside the fabric, remove and trim slightly.

4. Because it is small and easily manageable, this is an easy project for machine quilting. Simply follow the seam lines and stitch through all 3 layers of fabric.

   If you want to hand quilt, take small running stitches on each side of all seams.

To finish

1. Turn the raw edges of the top and bottom border strips $\frac{1}{4}$ inch to the inside and press.

2. Center one strip over the top of the quilt so that the raw edge of the quilt top is encased between the front and back of the strip. Pin together.

3. Repeat on the bottom edge.

4. Slipstitch the border edges to the front and back of the quilt on the top and bottom.

5. Use Velcro tabs to attach the quilt to the wall.

Figure 3

TIC TAC TOE

Each block of this quilt is made up of 9 patches in soft pink and green. This is a perfect quilt for using up scraps of light fabrics. The dark pieces of red and blue are added sparingly, here and there. This is a good size for a twin bed, but if you want something larger, simply add squares until you achieve the desired size. The overall look will be the same. The finished size of this pattern is 62½ × 73 inches.

Next Block

Jacobsladder
P 97

Table Cloth
P 141

Penwheel Star
P 82

~~IALS~~

~~rdages~~ are figured for fabric 45 inches wide. If you find home-
~~b~~ric 52 inches wide, you will need slightly less than indicated.

~~d~~s solid peach fabric (A)

~~s~~ aqua check fabric (B)

~~r~~ds peach plaid fabric (C)

~~r~~ds solid white fabric (D)

¾ yard aqua plaid fabric (E)

4⅛ yards backing fabric

thin quilt batting

DIRECTIONS

Note: All measurements include a ¼-inch seam allowance.

Cut the following

from peach (A):
    42 squares, each 6½ × 6½ inches

from aqua (B):
    22 squares, each 6½ × 6½ inches

from peach (C):
    42 squares, each 6½ × 6½ inches

from white (D):
    42 squares, each 6½ × 6½ inches

from aqua (E):
    20 squares, each 6½ × 6½ inches

To make a row

1. With right sides facing and raw edges aligned, stitch an A square to a
B square along one side edge. Open seam and press.

2. Continue to join squares according to the sequence below to make
12 rows of 14 squares each.

Row 1: A-B-C-D-A-E-C-D-A-B-C-D-A-E

Row 2: D-A-B-C-D-A-E-C-D-A-B-C-D-A

Row 3: C-D-A-B-C-D-A-E-C-D-A-B-C-D

Row 4: E-C-D-A-B-C-D-A-E-C-D-A-B-C

Row 5: A-E-C-D-A-B-C-D-A-E-C-D-A-B

Row 6: D-A-E-C-D-A-B-C-D-A-E-C-D-A

Row 7: C-D-A-E-C-D-A-B-C-D-A-E-C-D

Row 8: B-C-D-A-E-C-D-A-B-C-D-A-E-C

Row 9: A-B-C-D-A-E-C-D-A-B-C-D-A-E

Row 10: D-A-B-C-D-A-E-C-D-A-B-C-D-A

Row 11: C-D-A-B-C-D-A-E-C-D-A-B-C-D

Row 12: E-C-D-A-B-C-D-A-E-C-D-A-B-C

Joining rows

1. With right sides facing and raw edges aligned, stitch Row 1 to Row 2 along one long edge. Open seam and press.

2. Continue to join all 12 rows in this way.

To quilt

This project does not need quilting in order to be an attractive patchwork table cover. To finish without quilting, skip steps 3 and 4.

1. Cut the backing fabric in half. Stitch the 2 halves together lengthwise to create the backing.

2. With wrong sides facing and batting in between, pin the backing and patchwork top together.

3. Beginning at the center and working outward in a sunburst pattern, take long, loose stitches to baste the 3 layers of fabric together.

4. To hand quilt, start at the center of the quilt and take small running stitches ¼ inch on each side of all seam lines. To machine quilt, start at the center and stitch on all seam lines. *Stop stitching ½ inch from edge all around the quilt.*

To finish

1. Clip away all basting stitches.

2. Trim the batting ½ inch smaller than the quilt top all around.

3. Trim the backing to the same size as the quilt top.

4. Turn the raw edges of the backing and quilt top to the inside and press. Machine stitch all around to finish.

A	B	C	D	A	E	C	D	A	B	C	D	A	E
D	A	B	C	D	A	E	C	D	A	B	C	D	A
C	D	A	B	C	D	A	E	C	D	A	B	C	D
E	C	D	A	B	C	D	A	E	C	D	A	B	C
A	E	C	D	A	B	C	D	A	E	C	D	A	B
D	A	E	C	D	A	B	C	D	A	E	C	D	A
C	D	A	E	C	D	A	B	C	D	A	E	C	D
B	C	D	A	E	C	D	A	B	C	D	A	E	C
A	B	C	D	A	E	C	D	A	B	C	D	A	E
D	A	B	C	D	A	E	C	D	A	B	C	D	A
C	D	A	B	C	D	A	E	C	D	A	B	C	D
E	C	D	A	B	C	D	A	E	C	D	A	B	C

Figure 1

ROSES AND BOWS

This is an extremely easy quilt to make because large squares are used to piece the top. Setting each square on the diagonal makes it interesting. The floral motif in blue and white with splashes of pink roses will create a romantic bedroom retreat. The wide border, made from a contrasting overall printed fabric, frames the quilt. The 54-inch-wide chintz fabric is from the Waverly Collection and can be ordered through most fabric shops.

Each white square has a bow that is made from the border fabric and stitched to the center to break up the large white areas. The finished quilt is 82×104 inches and is ample for a double or queen-size bed.

MATERIALS

Note: Yardages for rose print and the white fabric are figured for fabrics 54 inches wide. Backing and border fabrics can be 45 inches wide.

2¾ yards white fabric (A)

2¾ yards rose print (B)

3 yards overall print for borders

6 yards backing fabric

quilt batting

DIRECTIONS

Note: All measurements include a ¼-inch seam allowance.

Cut the following

from white:

       inside border—

       2 strips, each 2½ × 66½ inches for top and bottom

       2 strips, each 2½ × 92½ inches for sides

    12 squares, each 16 × 16 inches

from rose print:

      6 squares, each 16 × 16 inches

      5 squares, each 16½ × 16½ inches; cut each square in half on the diagonal to make 10 triangles

      2 squares, each 17 × 17 inches; cut each square into 4 triangles (for the corners)

from overall print:

      borders—

      2 strips, each 6½ × 104½ inches

      2 strips, each 6½ × 70½ inches

    12 strips, each 2 × 12 inches for the bows (optional)

To make a row

Refer to Figure 1.

1. With right sides facing and raw edges aligned, stitch one short edge of large rose B triangle to each side edge of a white A square. Open seams and press.

2. Next, stitch the long edge of a small rose B triangle to the top edge of the white square in Row 1. Open seam and press.

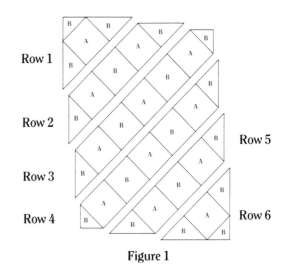

Figure 1

3. Continue to make all 6 rows according to Figure 1. Open seams and press.

Joining rows

1. With right sides facing and raw edges aligned, stitch Row 1 to Row 2 along the long edge. Open seam and press.

2. Continue to join all 6 rows in this way.

Borders

Refer to Figure 2.

1. With right sides facing and raw edges aligned, stitch a white 2½ × 66½-inch strip to the top edge of the quilt top. Open seam and press.

2. Repeat on the bottom edge.

3. With right sides facing and raw edges aligned, stitch a white 2½ × 92½-inch strip to each side edge of the quilt in the same way.

4. With right sides facing and raw edges aligned, stitch a printed 6½ × 70½-inch strip to the top edge of the quilt top. Open seams and press.

5. Repeat on the bottom edge.

6. Next, stitch a printed 6½ × 104½-inch strip to each side of the quilt in the same way.

To quilt

This quilt is quite pretty as a patchwork project without any hand quilting. If you prefer not to quilt, omit steps 2 and 3.

1. With wrong sides facing and batting in between, pin the top, batting, and backing together.

2. Starting at the center and working outward in a sunburst pattern, baste with long, loose stitches.

3. To hand quilt, take small running stitches ¼ inch on each side of all seam lines. To machine quilt, run the stitches along the seam lines. This is a large amount of fabric to work under the machine and it will have to be done carefully. Start at the center and work to the outside edges. *Stop stitching ½ inch from the outside edges all around.*

To finish

1. Trim the batting ½ inch smaller than the quilt top all around.

2. Trim the backing to the same size as the quilt top.

3. Turn the raw edges of the quilt top ¼ inch to the inside and press.

4. Turn the raw edges of the backing to the inside and press.

5. Pin the front and back edges together and machine stitch all around.

Bows

1. With *wrong* sides facing, fold each of the 12 strips in half lengthwise and press.

2. Clip each end at a 45-degree angle. Turn all raw edges to the inside and press. Stitch together.

3. Tie each strip into a ribbon bow. Center a bow on each white square and pin in place.

4. To secure each bow, bring the needle up from the underside of the quilt (as you would for quilting) through all 3 layers of fabric and through the center of the tied bow. Take several stitches in this way to hold each bow in place and to secure the backing and batting to the quilt top. This is a slight variation of a traditionally tied quilt.

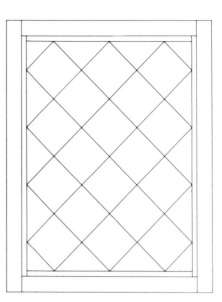

Figure 2

IRISH CHAIN

The Irish Chain is one of the most frequently reproduced early American quilt patterns, and understandably so. It's a simple country design that's always appealing. It's also easy to make with the strip-piecing method, a quick shortcut for piecing small squares. For a bold graphic design, you can combine any solid color with a white background, or combine calico prints for a country quilt. For this quilt, we used a predominantly white background fabric with a subtle overall blue print to match the blue calico squares.

This quilt was designed by my daughter Robby, who did the patchwork. I did the hand quilting in the evenings while relaxing. It was an easy project to quilt because I simply followed the seam lines and then quilted all the squares with an X from corner to corner. The finished size is 63×81 inches.

MATERIALS

Note: Yardages are figured for fabric 45 inches wide.

1½ yards blue calico fabric

3½ yards white with blue calico fabric

3¾ yards backing fabric

quilt batting

water-soluble quilt marker

ruler

DIRECTIONS

Note: All measurements include a ¼-inch seam allowance.

Cut the following

from blue:

    15 strips, each 3½ × 42 inches

from white:

    12 strips, each 3½ × 42 inches

    31 squares, each 9½ × 9½ inches

Strip piecing

Refer to Figure 1.

1. With right sides facing and raw edges aligned, stitch a blue strip to the long top edge of a white strip. Open seam and press.

2. Repeat on the long bottom edge. Make 6 sets of strips in this way.

3. Cut into 3½-inch segments as shown in Figure 1. You will need 64 of the 72 segments.

4. With right sides facing and raw edges aligned, stitch a white strip to the top edge of a blue strip. Open seam and press.

5. Repeat on the bottom edge. Make 3 sets of strips in this way.

6. Cut into 3½-inch segments. Make 32.

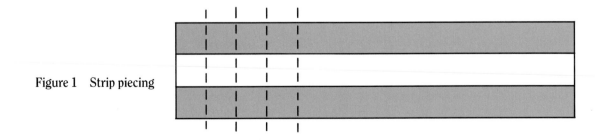

Figure 1   Strip piecing

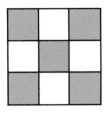

Figure 2

To make a block

Refer to Figure 2.

1. With right sides facing and raw edges aligned, stitch a blue/white/ blue segment to a white/blue/white segment, followed by a blue/white/ blue segment.

2. Open seams and press. Make 32 blocks in this way.

To make a row

Refer to Figure 3.

Row 1

1. With right sides facing and raw edges aligned, stitch a block to the left side of a white square. Open seam and press.

2. Next, join another block to the opposite side of the white square.

3. Continue to join blocks, alternating with white squares to make a row of 4 blocks, separated by 3 white squares.

4. Open seams and press. Make 5 rows in this way.

Row 2

1. With right sides facing and raw edges aligned, stitch a white square to the left side of a block. Open seam and press.

2. Next, join another white square to the opposite side of the block.

3. Continue to join squares and blocks until you have a row of 4 squares and 3 blocks.

4. Open seams and press. Make 4 rows in this way.

Joining rows

Refer to Figure 3.

1. With right sides facing and raw edges aligned, stitch Row 1 to Row 2. Open seam and press.

2. Continue to join rows, alternating Row 1 with Row 2 until you have joined all 9 rows.

3. Open seams and press.

Figure 3

To quilt

1. Use the ruler and quilt pen to mark off the quilting lines. Draw diagonal lines, from corner to corner, through all the large and small squares on the pieced quilt top.

2. Cut the backing fabric in half and stitch the 2 pieces together lengthwise to make a piece large enough to cover the back of the quilt.

3. With wrong sides facing and the batting in between, pin the top and backing together.

4. Starting in the center and working outward in a sunburst pattern, take long, loose basting stitches through all 3 layers of fabric.

5. Following all premarked quilting lines, take small running stitches. Quilt ¼ inch on each side of all seam lines as well. *End stitching ½ inch from the outside edges all around.*

To finish

1. Remove all basting stitches. Use a plant mister or damp sponge to remove all quilt lines.

2. Trim the backing ½ inch larger than the quilt top all around.

3. Trim the batting ½ inch smaller than the quilt top all around.

4. Turn the raw edges of the backing ¼ inch to the inside and press.

5. Bring the remaining ¼ inch of the backing over onto the quilt top and press. Pin and slipstitch or machine stitch all around to finish.

STRIPES AND SOLIDS

One of the easiest quilts in the book, this one is made up of large patchwork squares sewn together in rows. A border of one of the fabrics is added all around. The interest comes from the use of fabric, a solid green with solid white and a stripe of green and white, to create a bold, two-color design. This quilt was made for us by Diane Lewis of Boca Raton, Florida. The cool colors are perfect for a tropical climate.

The finished size is 64 × 88 inches, just right for a single bed. To make the quilt larger for a double bed, simply add more squares to the rows and another border of one of the other fabrics until you have the desired size.

MATERIALS

Note: Yardages are figured for fabric 45 inches wide.

¾ yard light-green fabric (A)

¾ yard white fabric (B)

2½ yards dark-green fabric (C)

¾ yard green-and-white striped fabric (D)

3¾ yards backing fabric

quilt batting

DIRECTIONS

Note: All measurements include a ¼-inch seam allowance.

Cut the following

from light green (A):

    24 squares, each 6½ × 6½ inches

from white (B):

    24 squares, each 6½ × 6½ inches

from dark green (C):

    borders—

    2 strips, each 8½ × 48½ inches (top and bottom
      borders)

    2 strips, each 8½ × 88½ inches (side borders)

    24 squares, each 6½ × 6½ inches

from striped fabric (D):

    24 squares, each 6½ × 6½ inches

To make a row

Note: When joining squares to make up the rows, be sure to follow the diagram for placement of squares in each row, taking special care with the horizontal and vertical placement of the striped fabric.

1. With right sides facing and raw edges aligned, join an A square to a B square along one side edge. Open seams and press.

2. Next, join a C square, then a D square, followed by an A, then B, then C, ending with a D square. Open all seams and press.

3. Continue to make rows following the sequence below. You will have a total of 12 rows of 8 squares each.

    Row 2: B-C-D-A-B-C-D-A

    Row 3: C-D-A-B-C-D-A-B

    Row 4: D-A-B-C-D-A-B-C

    Row 5: A-B-C-D-A-B-C-D

    Row 6: B-C-D-A-B-C-D-A

    Row 7: C-D-A-B-C-D-A-B

    Row 8: D-A-B-C-D-A-B-C

    Row 9: A-B-C-D-A-B-C-D

    Row 10: B-C-D-A-B-C-D-A

    Row 11: C-D-A-B-C-D-A-B

    Row 12: D-A-B-C-D-A-B-C

4. Open all seams and press.

A	B	C	D	A	B	C	D
B	C	D	A	B	C	D	A
C	D	A	B	C	D	A	B
D	A	B	C	D	A	B	C
A	B	C	D	A	B	C	D
B	C	D	A	B	C	D	A
C	D	A	B	C	D	A	B
D	A	B	C	D	A	B	C
A	B	C	D	A	B	C	D
B	C	D	A	B	C	D	A
C	D	A	B	C	D	A	B
D	A	B	C	D	A	B	C

Figure 1

 A × 24   B × 24   C × 24   D × 24

To join rows

1. With right sides facing and all seams aligned, pin Row 1 to Row 2 and stitch along the bottom edge. Open seam and press.

2. Continue to join rows in this way, making sure all seam lines match perfectly.

Borders

1. With right sides facing and raw edges aligned, pin the 8½ × 48½-inch dark-green top border strip to the top edge of the pieced quilt top.

2. Stitch together along the top edge. Open seam and press. Repeat on the bottom edge of the quilt.

3. Join the dark-green 8½ × 88½-inch side borders in the same way.

To prepare backing

1. Cut the fabric in half.

2. With right sides facing, stitch these 2 pieces together along one side edge.

3. Trim the backing about 2–3 inches larger than the quilt top all around.

To quilt

1. Pin the quilt top to the quilt batting and then to the backing fabric.

2. Starting at the center and working outward in a sunburst pattern, take long basting stitches through all 3 layers of fabric. The basting lines should be about 6 inches apart.

3. Hand stitching always looks best for quilting, but if you want to do this on the machine to save time, loosen the tension and set stitches to about 6–8 to the inch. Stitch along all seam lines on the quilt top. *Stop stitching within ½ inch of the edges all around.*

4. *For hand quilting:* Take small running stitches ¼ inch on each side of all seam lines through all 3 layers of fabric. *Do not stitch into ½-inch seam allowance all around quilt.*

To finish

1. Clip away all basting stitches.

2. Turn raw edges of the backing and top fabrics ¼ inch to the inside and press. Pin all around.

3. Machine stitch around the quilt, close to the outside edge.

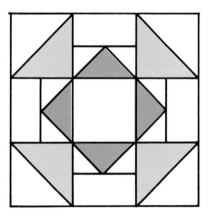

HANDY ANDY

The use of pastel solids with white gives this quilt a light and airy feeling. The calico border frames it and adds interest. The blocks for this pattern are made of 6-inch squares for quick-and-easy piecing. While this quilt was made for a single bed, you can easily enlarge it by adding another row of blocks or making the borders wider. This quilt measures 64 × 86 inches and was made for us by Corrinne Allesandrello.

MATERIALS

Note: Yardages are figured for fabric 45 inches wide.

½ yard pink fabric

½ yard aqua fabric

2½ yards white fabric

2½ yards blue calico fabric

4 yards backing fabric (we used white)

quilt batting

tracing paper

water-soluble fabric marker

DIRECTIONS

Note: All measurements include a ¼ inch seam allowance.

Cut the following

from pink:

> 12 squares, each 7 × 7 inches; cut each square into 2 triangles (24 triangles)

from aqua

> 12 squares, each 5¼ × 5¼ inches; cut each square into 2 triangles (24 triangles)

from white:

> borders—
> 2 strips, each 2½ × 74½ inches (sides)
> 2 strips, each 2½ × 48½ inches (top and bottom)
> 12 squares, each 7 × 7 inches; cut each square into 2 triangles (24 triangles)

> 6 squares, each 6½ × 6½ inches

> 24 squares, each 4 × 4 inches; cut each square into 2 triangles (48 triangles)

> 4 rectangles, each 3½ × 6½ inches

from blue calico:

> borders—
> 2 strips, each 6½ × 86½ inches (outer sides)
> 2 strips, each 6½ × 52½ inches (outer top and bottom)
> 2 side lattice strips, each 4½ × 70½ inches

Handy Andy quilting pattern for outside border.

INDEX

Allesandrello, Corrine, 159
Amish 9 Patch, 95
Around the World, 71

Baby Blocks, 70
Baby Stripes, 54
backing, 9
Barn Raising, 100
basting, 9, 15
batting, 9, 11
Bear Claw, 118
binding, 9
block, 9
Blue and White Missouri Star, 32
borders, 9

Card Trick, 20
corner edge,
    inside, 14
    outside, 14
curves, 14
cutting board, 12

enlarging designs, 13
estimating fabric yardage, 12

fabric, 10
    Laura Ashley, 54
    Waverly, 20, 89, 143
Fair and Square, 26

getting started in quilting, 8-18
grid patterns, 10, 12

hand quilting, 15, 18
Handy Andy, 159
hanging a quilt, 17
Harlequin Squares, 58
Homespun Table Cover, 139
how to quilt, 15-16

inside corner edge, 14
Introduction, 5
Irish Chain, 148
iron, 12

Jacob's Ladder, 89
Joyce, Susan Fernald, 25, 42, 100

Kaleidoscope, 129

Laura Ashley, 54
LeMoyne Star, 63
Lewis, Diane, 154
Log Cabin Wall Hanging, 76

machine quilting, 15
making a template, 13
markers, 12
materials for quilting, 10-12
Maze of Grays, 48

needles, 11, 18

Odell, Deborah, 76, 129
outlining, 16
outside corner edge, 14
overall quilting, 12, 16

patchwork, 10
patterns,
    Around the World, 71
    Bear Claw, 118
    Log Cabin, 76, 129
Peluso, Peter, Jr., 32, 89
piecing, 10
piecing the backing, 13
pillows, 89, 124
Pinwheel Star, 82
points, 14

quick-and-easy methods, 16-17
quilting, 10-16
    by hand, 15
    by machine, 15
    grids, 12
    patterns, 10-16, 18
    techniques, 12-16
    terms, 9-10
quilts
    quick, 26, 48, 54, 89, 113, 124,
        143, 148, 154, 159
    traditional, 63, 82, 89, 118, 148
    unique fabric, 20, 38, 48, 113,
        124, 139, 143

removing pencil marks, 18
right triangles, 16
Roman Stripes, 42
Roses and Bows, 143
ruler, 12

sash or strips, 10
Schumaker, F. & Company, 20
scissors, 11
setting, 10
sewing
    curves, 14
    inside a corner edge, 14
    outside corner edge, 14
    points, 14
sewing tips, 18
Skinner, Avis, 48
Smith, Robby, 5, 6, 7, 71, 148
Stearns, Jane and Scott, 95
strip piecing, 16
Stripes and Solids, 154
Summer Coverlet, 124

tablecloths, 20, 124, 139
template, 11, 18
thimble, 11
thread, 11
Tic Tac Toe, 134
top, 10
transferring a large design, 13
triangle method, quick-and-easy, 16
triangles, right, 16
turning corners, 14

Vis-à-Vis, 48
    Collection, 63

wall hangings, 20, 42, 71, 76, 95, 100,
    129
Waverly Collection, 143
Waverly Fabric, 20, 89, 143
Wedding Wreath, 107
White on White, 113
Wool Coverlet, 38

yardage,
    estimating, 12
yardstick, 12

All of us at Sedgewood® Press are dedicated to offering you, our customer, the best books we can create. We are particularly concerned that all of the instructions for making the projects are clear and accurate. We welcome your comments and would like to hear any suggestions you may have. Please address your correspondence to Customer Service Department, Sedgewood® Press, Meredith Corporation, 750 Third Avenue, New York, NY 10017.

For information on how you can have *Better Homes and Gardens* delivered to your door, write to: Mr. Robert Austin, P.O. Box 4536, Des Moines, IA 50336.